CW01660422

Home Automation Projects with Arduino

Using the RFID Starter kit

All components required for these experiments are contained in the RFID Starter kit

Günter Spanner

an Elektor Publication

LEARN | DESIGN | SHARE

This is an Elektor Publication. Elektor is the media brand of
Elektor International Media B.V.
78 York Street, London W1H 1DP, UK
Phone: (+44) (0)20 7692 8344

British Library Cataloguing in Publication Data
A catalogue record for this book is available from the British Library

ISBN 978-1-907920-60-8

Prepress Production: D-Vision, Julian van den Berg
First published in the United Kingdom 2017
Printed in the Netherlands by Wilco

Introduction

Without doubt the Arduino system has become 'the' basic component amongst electronics communities and makers. Earlier it was necessary to begin with a bare microcontroller as the basic building block of any system, now the Arduino is more and more frequently used. Armed with the Arduino system your first steps into the world of microcontroller technology could not be made any simpler. Instead of a complex programming environment, where you would be expected to start coding from scratch you can now work with a highly intuitive development environment combining pre-tested library routines to get you up and running in no time.

When it comes to plugging in additional hardware to the basic Arduino board the developer is still largely on their own. There is a wealth of special expansion boards for the Arduino but these are often only useful for some specific application areas. If you really want to build some innovative projects you often have to get down to component level. This presents many beginners with major problems.

There are some developer's kits which can help in this area. These contain a range of components that you can use with the Arduino to build lots of different projects and help you understand how they work.

That is exactly the purpose of this book. It explains how a wealth of practical projects can be built from a single kit. This kit, called the 'RFID Starter Kit for Arduino UNO' contains more than 30 components, devices and modules from all areas of modern electronics.

In addition to more simple components such as LEDs and resistors there are also complex and sophisticated modules that use the latest technology such as:

- A humidity sensor
- A multicolor LED
- A large LED matrix with 64 points of light
- A 4-character 7-segment LED display
- An infra red remote-controller unit
- A complete LC-display module

Additional special devices include:

- A servo
- A stepper motor and controller module
- A complete RFID reader module and security tag

With these components you can build a whole lot of different projects. For the beginner, we first start off with a few simple introductory experiments. More experienced users can on the other hand go on to build the more complex projects that are described a bit later in the book.

In addition to precise digital thermometers, hygrometers, exposure meters and various alarm systems, there are also practical devices and applications such as

- A fully automatic plant irrigation system
- A sound-controlled remote control system
- A digital clock with versatile display possibilities
- A multifunctional weather station

plus much more.

The projects presented here could not be classed as 'laboratory prototypes' but are instead practical and useful designs, fully described with lots of hints and tips on their use in hobby, household and professional applications.

All the projects can be built using the components supplied in the Elektor kit. Alternatively, most of the components can also be purchased from specialist dealers or from online auction sites. At the end of the book a description of these components and a source from where they can be purchased is given. With this information you can replace defective or lost components.

This also gives you the option to purchase components to build individual projects without the the need for the entire kit. The SainSmart Boards have also been offering a cost-effective yet high-quality Arduino clone for some time now. Their boards are fully compatible with the classic Arduinos.

All the sketches given in this book are available to download from:

www.elektor.com

When the sketch is not identical to the listing in this book the downloaded version will be the latest version and is the one that should be used.

Chapter 1 • A quick introduction to the Hard- and Software

In general, 'Arduino' can be used to refer to the development board itself, i.e. the hardware of which there are now many variants of the original Arduino board but we will go into that in a little more detail below. Arduino also refers to the programming environment, together they make up the 'Arduino System'.

The Arduino hardware consists of a microcontroller board. This is a circuit board or PCB on which there are several other electronic components besides the microcontroller itself.

Along the two long edges of the board the Arduino has a row of header sockets commonly referred to in the text as the Arduino's pins. The pins are used to connect the various electronic components to the Arduino. These components, eg pushbuttons, Light Emitting Diodes (LEDs), various sensors, potentiometers, displays, motors, servos etc. will all be used in the following chapters.
There are now lots of different versions of Arduino boards which can be used with the Arduino software. This includes boards of different size all labelled with the official 'Arduino' or 'Genuino' logo.

In addition to the official series of boards there are a number of unofficial third party boards or clones which are substantially cheaper than the originals. They are largely compatible in terms of both hardware and software which means that electrically they produce the same signals and they can be programmed with the Arduino IDE.

The classic Arduino controller boards have names like:

- Arduino UNO,
- Arduino MEGA,
- Arduino Micro etc.

While their corresponding clones have names such as:

- Seeduino UNO,
- Funduino MEGA,
- Freeduino Micro
- SainSmart UNO etc.

The Arduino UNO (see below) is used throughout this book for all of the projects described here. One important compatible board called the SainSmart UNO, can also be substituted for the original Arduino in all the projects.

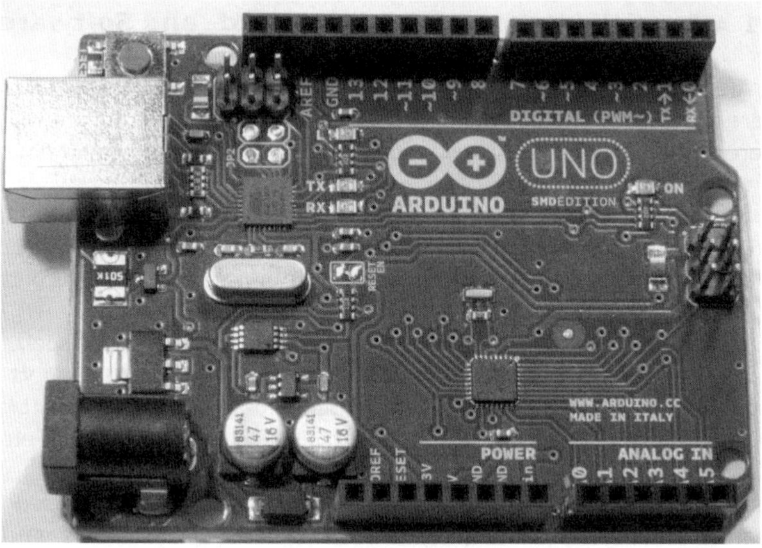

Illustration 1: An original Arduino UNO

In addition to all the electronic components in the kit there are also a bunch of jumper wires that are used for making fast and flexible connections between the Arduino and other components. The flexible cable has a stiff pin at each end for it to plug into the Arduino header strips. Their flexibility makes it easy connect up large structures. Using these wires eliminates the need for time-consuming soldering. They also plug into the protyping plug board or breadboard that we make use of here to build up more complex circuits.

Their flexibility allows you to test projects and devices without having to make and unsolder joints repeateadly. This construction method has gained broad acceptance in the wider Arduino community.

Once the circuit idea has been tested you might wish to make a more permanent version of the circuit using either perf board or a proper custom-made PCB.

The prototyping breadboard or plug board is a really useful base on which to build up circuits. It's particularly good for teaching and training and once the circuit has been tested and understood all the components and wires can just be unplugged and re-used later. With careful handling the plug board and accessories will last a long time.
The following illustration shows the structure of a breadboard. The lines indicate how the contacts are connected to each other. This arrangement makes the electrical connections between components and jumpers leads plugged into the board without the need for screws or solder.

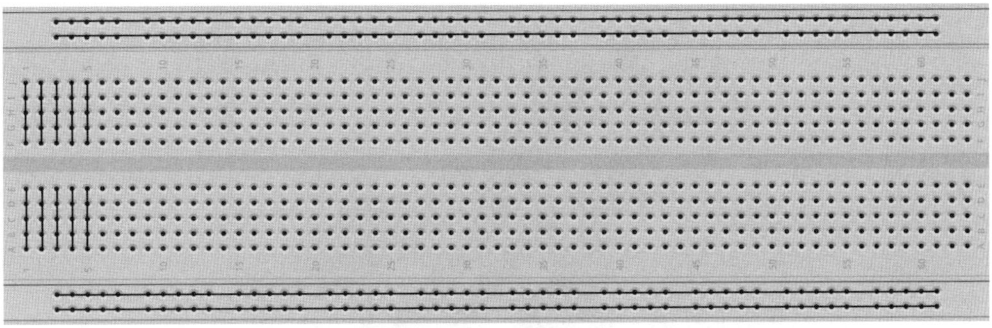

Illustration 2: Prototyping or Breadboard

The Breadboard is made of non conductive plastic with a matrix of holes at a pitch of 0.1 inch; underneath the holes are lines of conductive metal spring contacts. The complete board consists of three mains areas:

- The main plug field
- Two supply line strips

The main plug field is made up of strips of five plug rows (shown as vertical black lines in the illustration) covering the whole field. Any component or wire plugged into a strip will connect with anything else plugged into the other four positions. The two supply lines or power bus strips usually extend the whole length along the edge of the board; however some types may have a break at the centre of the board (indicated by a slightly longer gap between the lines of plug points). In this case you will need to bridge the break with some wire jumpers if you want the supply to be available over the full length of the board. Prototyping boards are available in several different sizes.
NB: Thin wires can easily get bent as you plug them in. Try to make sure that component wires are introduced vertically into the holes in the board.

With a new prototyping board the contacts can be a little stiff at first, it may be worth poking a pin in just to open them a few times so that components can more easily be inserted. Don't overdo it though otherwise you could end up with flaky contacts.

The Arduino connects to a PC or laptop via a standard A-B USB cable. This cable is also included in the hardware kit.

Illustration 3: The USB cable for the Arduino and PC or laptop

1.1 The first Functional Test

LEDs are really useful for quickly showing some test results of a project. They are therefore used in almost all Arduino projects. In principle, LEDs are pretty robust components, but you need to take into account some basic things before you start using them for the first time:

- The current can only flow in one direction through an LED. Make sure it is connected the correct way round! An LED has two leads; one lead is shorter than the other. For current to flow the longer lead connects to the more positive (+) point while the shorter lead connects to the more negative (-) point in the circuit.

- When the LED is connected to a constant voltage supply (such as a battery) you must also connect a resistor in series with the LED to limit the current otherwise it will be quickly destroyed. An LED powered from a 5 V supply must have a resistor with a minimum resistance of 220 Ohm connected in series. One of the ten **220 Ohm resistors in the kit could be used for this purpose.**

Light emitting diodes or LEDs are usually used in microcontroller technology to display port states. As well as a shorter lead the LED cathode (which connects to the more negative voltage) will also be marked with a flat on its plastic housing.

The kit contains the following selection of LEDs:

- 5x LED red,
- 5x LED green
- 5x LED yellow

That's 15 LEDs altogether. The LEDs are intended for use at a supply current of 20 mA.

Armed with this knowledge we can build our first test circuit. The following illustration shows how to use an LED with a series resistor on an Arduino. A 220 Ohm resistor is used in series with the LED. Depending on the type of resistor it will be marked with colored bands to show its value of resistance, the sequence of bands will either be

red – red – brown - gold

or

red – red – black – black - brown

That there are two different versions is due to the construction of the resistance. The standard carbon film resistors usually have a brown body and three colored bands. There may be a fourth gold or silver band. The higher-quality metal film resistors usually have a blue body and five colored bands. If the circuit is configured correctly, the Arduino can be connected to a PC or laptop via a USB cable. In addition to the LEDs on the Arduino itself, the external LED should now also light up brightly when the USB cable is plugged in.

Tip: When the LED does not light up just try switching its connections!

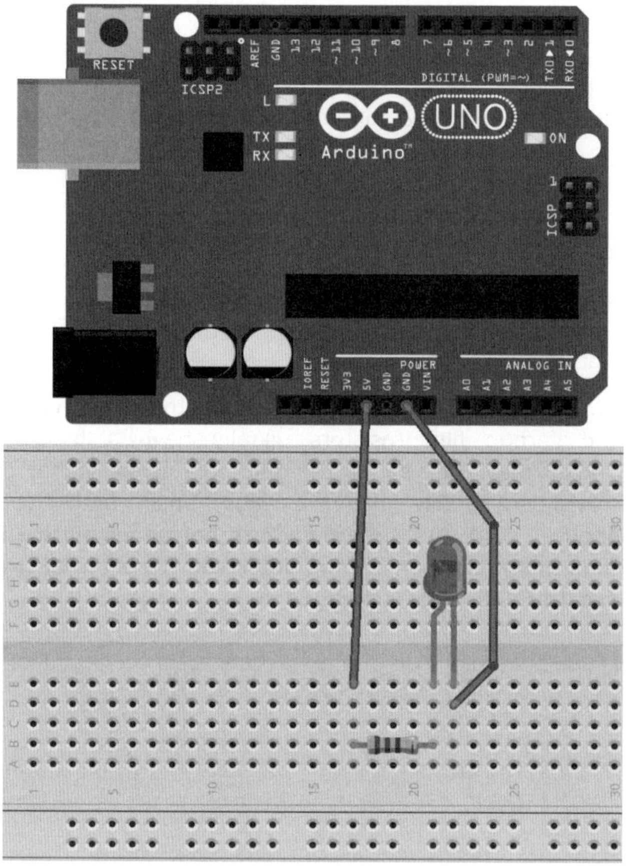

Illustration 4: An LED and Arduino

1.2 Programming the Arduino

The software with which the microcontroller is programmed is open-source software and can be found at:

www.arduino.cc

From where it can be downloaded free of charge from the Internet. In this 'Arduino programming environment' the programs are created, which the Arduino microcontroller executes later. In the Arduino environment, a program is generally referred to as a 'sketch'.
If you have a reliable Internet connection, you can also use the online IDE (Arduino Web Editor). It allows you to save your sketches in the cloud so you can access them from wherever you may be and have them available from any device and also backed up. This option ensures you'll always have the most up-to-date version of the IDE without the need to install updates or community generated libraries.
For all the projects described here we use the Arduino IDE build 1.6.5 installed on a Windows PC. The Arduino build version 1.6.6 includes a Serial Plotter feature as well as the Serial Monitor. It is like a low bandwidth oscilloscope, good for display waveforms. We make

use of this feature later on in the projects.
Using this installed IDE finished sketches can be transferred from the Arduino programming environment to the Arduino board using a USB cable. First, however, the Arduino software environment and possibly one of the USB drivers must be installed in the PC for the board. There are two options for downloading the software environment:

- The Installer
- The ZIP files

The first one installs everything you need to use the Arduino Software Environment (IDE) straight away, including the drivers. The second one with the Zip package you need to install the drivers manually in a directory.

NB: Do not connect the Arduino board to the PC yet!
Once the installation is complete, open the software folder containing the Arduino system and double click on the arduino.exe file to open the IDE. Next there are two important settings to check to make sure everthing is correctly configured.
First check under 'Tools' that the correct type of Arduino board is chosen. A 'SainSmart Uno' board is identified as an 'Arduino/Genuino Uno'.

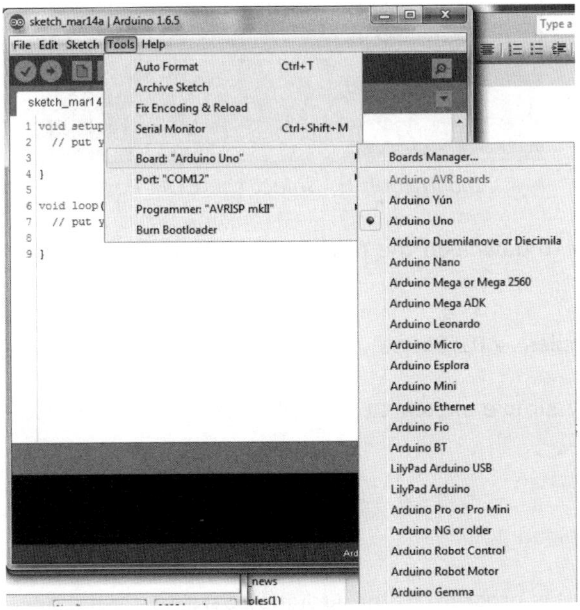

Illustration 5: Enter the correct board type

The next thing to check is the communication port number used by the PC to communicate with Arduino board.
Under the Tools tab click on Port where the serial connection is defined e.g.
The Arduino is now connected to the computer. A menu item will appear in the port se-

lection list, eg

COM3 (Arduino/Genuino Uno)

Click here to make the connection.

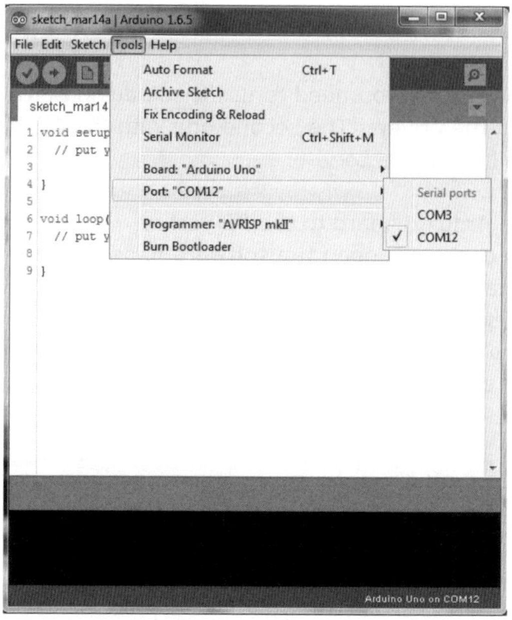

Illustration 6: Select the COM Port

The system is ready to download the first program to run on the board. Now click on the menu options:

File → Examples → 01.Basics → Blink

Which loads a really simple sketch to the IDE which when it is uploaded to the Arduino board blinks the LED.
Now select

Sketch → Upload

to compile and load this program to the Arduino board.
Once these steps have been taken correctly, the LED marked '13' or 'L' on the Arduino board will start flashing after the sketch is compiled and uploaded.
Now if we rewire the first circuit so that it looks like the next illustration, then the external LED will also flash at the same rhythm as the LED on the Arduino.
So your first program-controlled circuit is now working!

The illustrations and tests were implemented using the Arduino program build 1.6.5. in Windows 10. When using other versions or other operating system variants, slight variations may occur.

All the sketches in this book have been created and tested with this configuration. Usually, Arduino sketches are upwards compatible, which means that sketches created using older build versions of the IDE will also run on the new version. However, there are always exceptions to this rule. In case of problems, it is advisable to compile the sketches using version 1.6.5.

Note on installing a USB driver

In the configuration shown here there is no requirement to install any USB drivers. In earlier build versions however, it may be necessary to manually install such drivers. In this case, the PC will report that the connected board is recognized, but a driver still needs to be installed.

When this message does appear don't go blindly on. Often the reason for this is that the necessary driver is not recognized automatically. In the course of the installation you will need to select the driver yourself. It is located in the Arduino program folder in the subfolder 'Drivers'.

You can carry out a simple check to see if the driver is correctly installed in the PC by going to the Control Panel, System and Security then click on 'Device Manager' in System. When the installation is correct it should show the Arduino board listed here. Otherwise it will be shown as an 'Unknown USB Device' and marked with a yellow triangle and exclamation mark. In this case click on this message and select 'Update Driver Software'. Now you can go through the process to manually install it.

1.3 Resistors: A Basic Element of Electronics

Resistors are among the simplest electronic components. They are unpolarized so they are not fussy which way round they are connected and they are quite robust. The value of a resistor is given by colored bands on the body. Basic carbon film resistors usually have a tolerance of 5% and are marked with four colors. Three bands indicate their value of resistance; the fourth may be gold-colored indicating its value has a tolerance of 5%. The kit contains the high-quality metal film resistors. For this type with 1% tolerance, five colors are required to give the value; a brown fifth ring indicates a tolerance of 1%. The tolerance ring is usually slightly wider than the others. The hardware kit contains the following 30 resistors

- 10 x 220 Ohm
- 10 x 1k Ohm
- 10 x 10k Ohm

The 220 Ohm resistors are often used as series resistors for individual LEDs and for seven-segment displays operating at 5 V.

The other two values are used in a wide variety of applications. Their use is explained in the corresponding projects. The following table shows the color codes of the resistors used in the kit:

Value	Color Code 5%	Color Code 1%
220 Ohm	red – red - brown	Rot - red – black - black
1 Kiloohm	Brown – black- red	Brown – black - black - brown
10 Kiloohm	Brown – black - orange	Brown – black - black - red

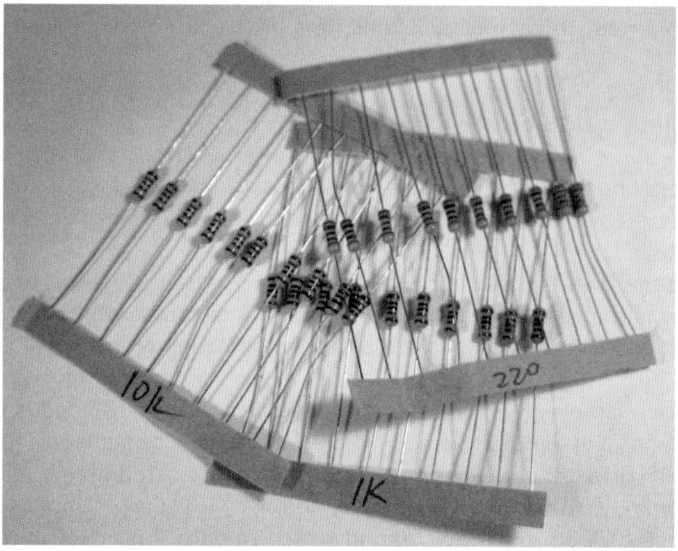

Illustration 7: Resistors

1.4 Are you well connected? Jumper cables

In order to make connections between individual electronic components, jumper cables are used. In the hardware kit there are a total of 65 jumper cables. These have different colors and different lengths. The following illustration shows some of these cables.

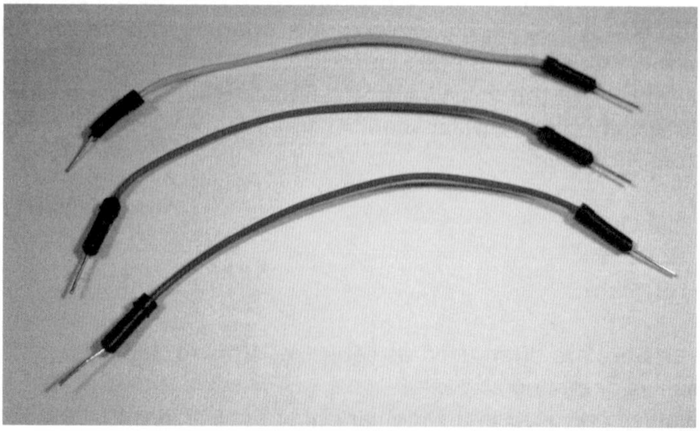

Illustration 8: Jumper cables

Also included in the kit are 10 'Female to Male' (F-M) jumper cables. At one end they have a 'male' plug that that fits into the holes of the breadboard. At the other end there is a socket ('female'). These cables are therefore always used when a board or module has pin connections, such as the keypad or RTC module.

Illustration 9: Male to Female cable

1.5 LEDs

The hardware kit contains 15 Light Emitting Diodes (LEDs) in red, yellow and green. These are used as indicator display units in various projects.

NB: An LED must always be connected in series with a resistor!
A resistor with a value of at least 220 Ohm must be used when the LED is operated from a 5 V supply.

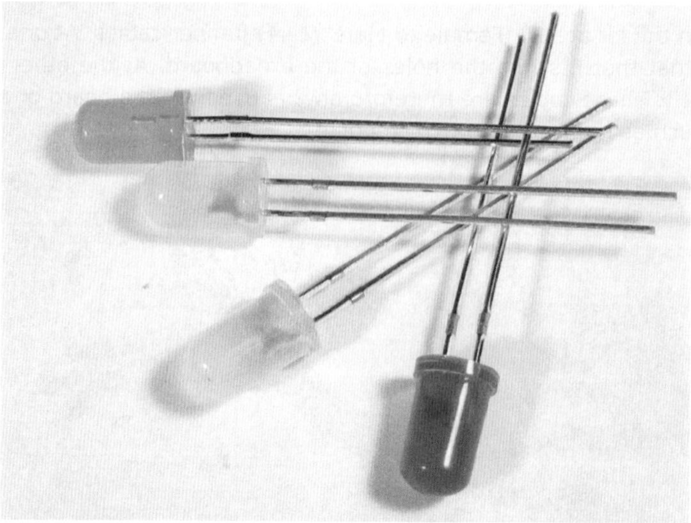

Illustration 10: LEDs Battery power for the Arduino

1.6 Battery power for the Arduino

During the normal program development phase the Arduino gets its supply voltage via the USB port. Once the application has been developed however the Arduino-based system can be unplugged from the PC or laptop and operated stand-alone from a battery. In this case, the 9V battery clip included in the kit can be used. After the clip is connected to a 9 V battery, the barrel plug can be inserted into the appropriate socket on the bottom left of the Arduino board. Now the board works on its own without a USB cable.

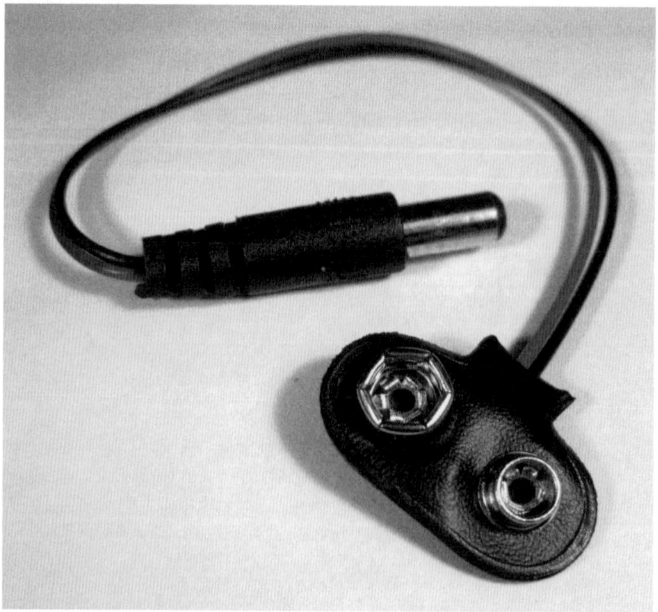

Illustration 11: The 9 V Battery clip

Chapter 2 • Fire up the Arduino - Projects for beginners

Now you have been introduced to all the components and the Arduino board has already been given a functional test the fun can begin. First off we start with some simple projects which you can build without the need for too much additional hardware. The accompanying sketches should also not cause any problems. They may be simple but working through the examples you will get to build many practical projects that you will find are very useful.

2.1 Alarm system simulator

Even this first simple project has a real practical use that could save you a great deal of stress. It is an alarm system simulator, useful as a burglar deterrent.
The most basic test program for the Arduino uses the blink.ino sketch. It makes an LED regularly flash on and off.
In this sketch called flash.ino the LED remains off for three seconds and then flashes briefly for a tenth of a second. This is a typical signal used by car and house alarm systems to indicate that the system is armed.
The flashing LED can be installed somewhere visible and with any luck it would deter an opportunist thief who would not know if this is a genuine signal from a sophisticated alarm system or just a decoy. Best of all, there's no risk of a false alarm waking you up at night!
The sketch looks like this:

```
// Alarm_simulator.ino

void setup()
{ pinMode(13, OUTPUT);
}

void loop()
{ digitalWrite(13, HIGH);    // turn the LED on (HIGH is the voltage level)
  delay(100);               // wait for a tenth of a second
  digitalWrite(13, LOW);    // turn the LED off by making the voltage LOW
  delay(3000);              // wait for three seconds
}
```

2.2 SOS Emergency signal

A single LED is all you need to generate an SOS signal. The three long followed by three short flashes is the internationally recognized signal to indicate distress. Bright LEDs can be seen from a distance and could be a life saver should you get lost on a mountain walk.

The signal is applied to the Arduino internal LED which is connected to digital pin D13 on the Uno. An external LED can be used connected to pin 12 for example, a 1K series resistor

```
int ledPin = 13; // LED in series with 1k resistor on pin 12
```

must be connected in series with pin D12 and the LED.

```
// SOS.ino

int ledPin = 13; // or external LED in series with 1k resistor on pin 12
int i;      // declare variable i

void setup()
{  pinMode(ledPin, OUTPUT);
}
void loop()
{  for (i=1; i <= 3; i++)
    {   digitalWrite(ledPin, HIGH);
        delay(500);
        digitalWrite(ledPin, LOW);
        delay(500);
    }
    delay(1000);
    for (i=1; i <= 3; i++)
    {   digitalWrite(ledPin, HIGH);
        delay(1500);
        digitalWrite(ledPin, LOW);
        delay(1500);
    }
    delay(1000);
    for (i=1; i <= 3; i++)
    {   digitalWrite(ledPin, HIGH);
        delay(500);
        digitalWrite(ledPin, LOW);
        delay(500);
    }
    delay(3000);
}
```

2.3 Mood lighting with a multicolor LED

As well as the standard range of LED indicator lamps which only light up in one color there is also the so-called multicolor LED. These contain three LED chips in one housing.

They normally contain a Red, Green and Blue LED. They also go by the name RGB LEDs. By controlling the on to off ratio of the signal switching each LED it's possible to produce not only the three basic colors but also all the color nuances in between, all the way up to white light.

When the colors change slowly in a predetermined sequence the effect is usually referred to as 'mood lighting'. Here is a sketch that produces this effect:

```
// Mood_light.ino

int ledRed = 6;
int ledGreen = 5;
int ledBlue = 3;

int colorWidth = 1000;

void setup()
{ }

void loop()
{ for(int fadeValue = 0 ; fadeValue <= 255; fadeValue ++)
  {
    analogWrite(ledRed, 255*exp(-((fadeValue-64)*(fadeValue-64))/
    colorWidth));
    analogWrite(ledGreen, 100*exp(-((fadeValue-128)*(fadeValue-128))/
    colorWidth));
    analogWrite(ledBlue, 200*exp(-((fadeValue-193)*(fadeValue-193))/
    colorWidth));
    delay(2);
  }
}
```

Changing the value of the 'colorWidth' parameter changes the color overlap and changing the delay function alters how quickly the colors change.

Illustration 12: The Multicolor LED module

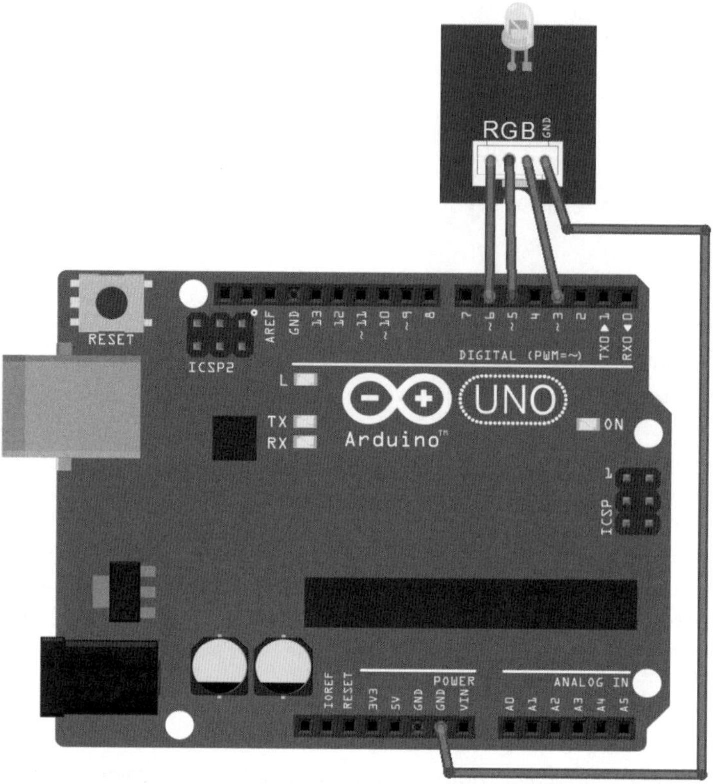

Illustration 13: Wiring the RGB-LED to the Arduino

2.4 Switches that Bounce

Using a microcontroller to read the state of something really basic like a pushbutton shows that it's not always as simple as you first thought. The following illustration shows how to connect a pushbutton to an Arduino.

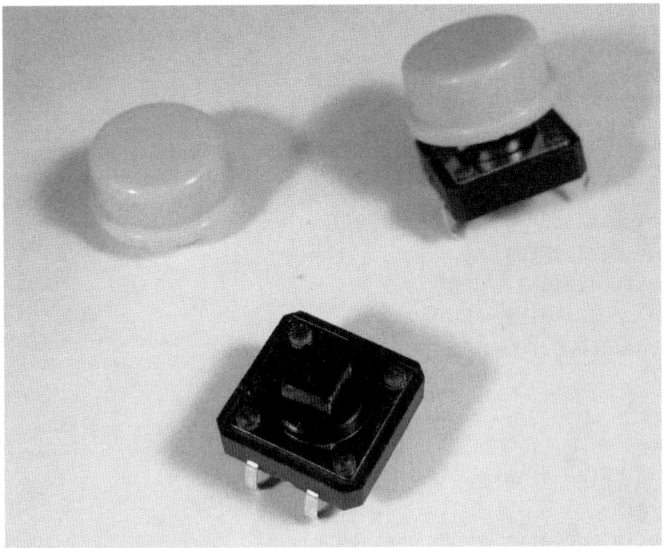

Illustration 14: pushbuttons and caps

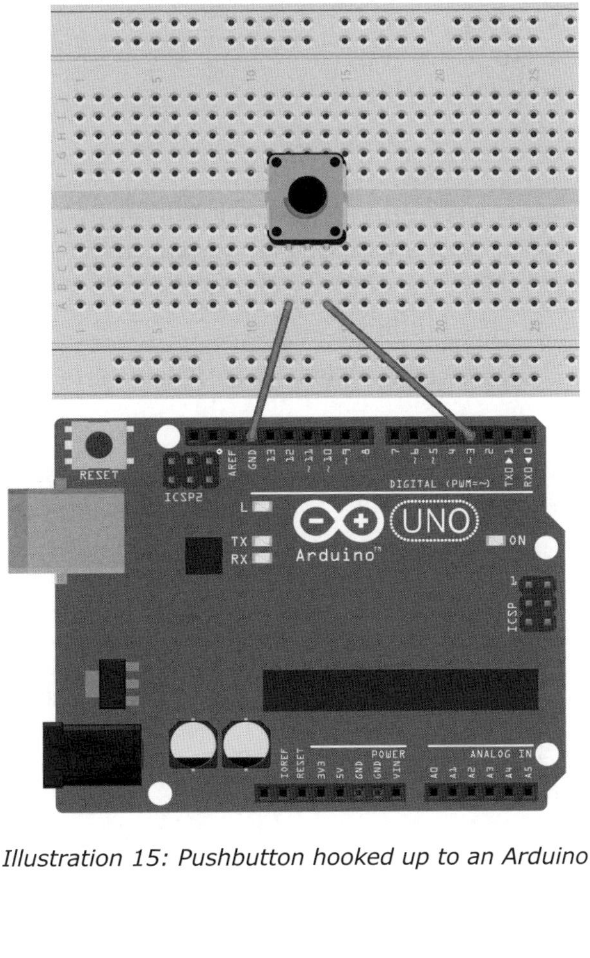

Illustration 15: Pushbutton hooked up to an Arduino

```
// Bouncing.ino

int SW1=3, LED=13;
int Toggle=0, n=0;

void setup()
{  Serial.begin(9600);
   pinMode(SW1,INPUT);
   digitalWrite(SW1,HIGH);
   Serial.println("Bouncing");
   pinMode(LED,OUTPUT);
}

void loop()
{ if(!digitalRead(SW1))
  {    n++;
       Serial.print("Switch pressed ");
       Serial.print(n,DEC);
       Serial.println(" times");
       Toggle=!Toggle;
       digitalWrite(LED,Toggle);
       do {} while(!digitalRead(SW1));
  }
}
```

While the program is running press the button and watch LED13 on the board and also the output on the Serial Monitor display (click on the Tools tab and select Serial Monitor). What value is given on the serial monitor display when you press the button ten times quickly in succession?

Chances are the count value is somewhere between 12 and 15!
What's going on?

Surely the displayed value of pushbutton presses should be the same as the number of times you pressed the button!

With the instruction

```
{ if(!digitalRead(SW1))
```

The program waits until the signal on pin 3 (connected to the pushbutton) goes low then the program carries on until it reaches

```
do {} while(!digitalRead(SW1));
```

Where it waits until the pushbutton is released.

How can it pass these conditional statements a number of times with just one press of the button?

The problem lies with the pushbutton itself (and for almost all mechanical switches). When the two contacts spring together they bounce back and forwards a few times before they settle down and become closed. Instead of a clean change from one state to another you actually get a series of pulses as the contacts bounce. Below you can see the waveform on the input pin of the Arduino viewed on an oscilloscope when the button's pressed. It's easy to spot the spike that the controller interprets as another button press. This problematic behavior afflicts most switches and is known as contact bounce.

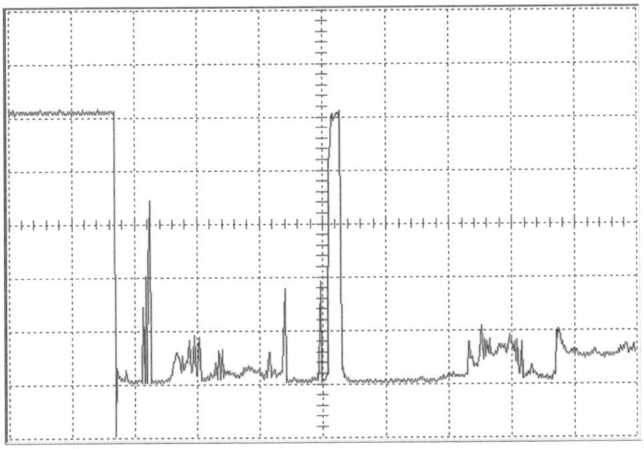

Illustration 16: Switch contact bounce

The problem can be solved in a number of different ways. In addition to using additional electronic hardware to solve the problem can also be solved in software by using whats known as a software debouncing routine.

In the following practical example a wait period of 50 ms is introduced after the first contact change is recognized before the contact is tested again. The contact input must have the same level during two successive reads before the software accepts this level as valid and increments the counter. Any level changes within this 50 ms 'window' are ignored.

The displayed value of pushbutton presses should now equal the number of times you actually pressed the button.

```
// Debouncing.ino

byte n=0;
int SW1=3;
int LED=13;
int Toggle=0;
```

```
byte value_1, value_2=0;


void setup()
{  Serial.begin(9600);
   pinMode(SW1,INPUT);
   digitalWrite(SW1,HIGH);
   pinMode(LED,OUTPUT);
   Serial.println("Debounce");
}

void loop()
{ value_1=digitalRead(SW1);
  if(!value_1)
  { delay(50);
    value_2=digitalRead(SW1);
    if(!value_2)
    { n++;
      Serial.print("Switch was pressed ");
      Serial.print(n,DEC);
      Serial.println(" times");
      Toggle=!Toggle;
      digitalWrite(LED,Toggle);
      do{}while(!digitalRead(SW1));
    }
  }
}
```

2.5 Data input using a keypad

Using a single pushbutton you can transfer simple information to the Arduino. To may want to enter more complex strings of information. In this case you can use a keyboard made up of several single keys. The hardware kit includes a 16-button keypad which can be used for a variety of applications.

The individual buttons are not wired separately but in the form of a matrix which requires fewer I/O signals to read the state of the buttons.

The buttons are wired according to this diagram:

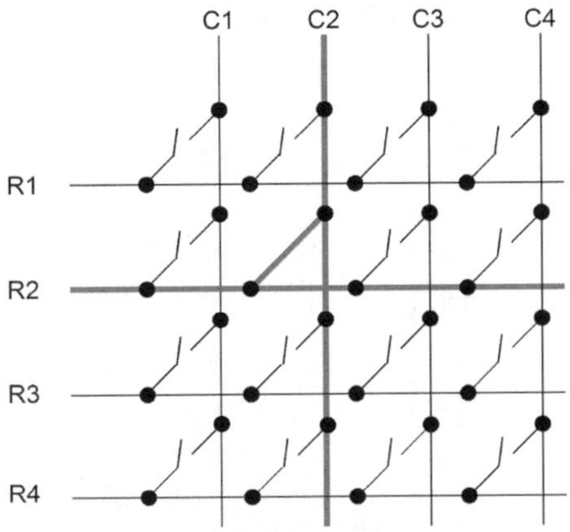

Illustration 17: How the keypad buttons are wired

Illustration 18: The Matrix keypad

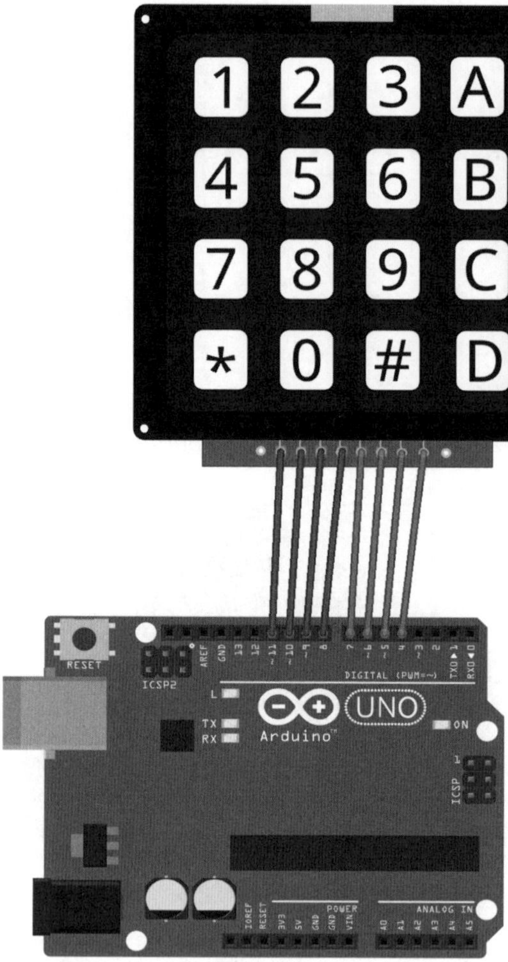

Illustration 19: Wiring the keypad to the Uno

The following table shows the keypad hook up:

Keypad	**Arduino**
Row 1	4
Row 2	5
Row 3	6
Row 4	7
Column 1	8
Column 2	9
Column 3	10
Column 4	11

For the necessary software to read the keypad we use a library for the first time. The library is available at

http://playground.arduino.cc/Code/Keypad#Download

to download from the internet free of charge.

The sketch to read the keypad looks like this:

```
// Keypad_4x4.ino

#include <Keypad.h>

char keys[4][4]={
 {'1','2','3','A'},
 {'4','5','6','B'},
 {'7','8','9','C'},
 {'*','0','#','D'}};

byte rowPin[4]={4,5,6,7};
byte colPin[4]={8,9,10,11};

Keypad keypad=Keypad(makeKeymap(keys),rowPin,colPin,4,4);

void setup()
{ Serial.begin(9600);
}

void loop()
{ char pressed=keypad.getKey();
 if(pressed)
 { Serial.print(pressed);
   Serial.print(", ");
 }
}
```

With the sketch running you can test the keypad operation. You will also need to click on the Serial Monitor button in the IDE. Click on the Tools tab and select Serial Monitor form the drop down menu.The start button for this is located in the upper right corner of the Arduino IDE:

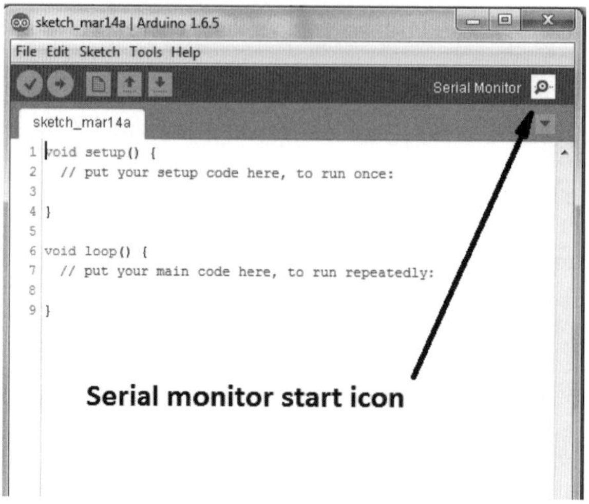

Illustration 20: The serial monitor start icon.

The result shown on the Serial Monitor display window should look like this:

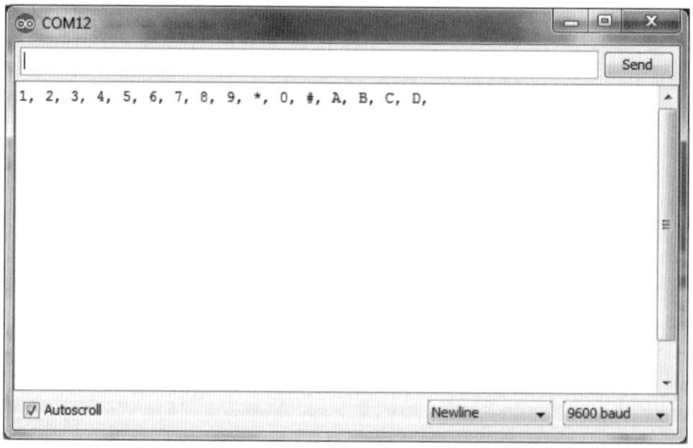

Illustration 21: Keypad press values in the serial monitor window

The keypad is used in chapter 8.8 in a project to build a code lock.

2.6 Warning signals of every pitch

You often want to produce data or output signal you can hear as well as see. This is also possible with the Arduino without much trouble.

A simple sound transducer can be used to convert electrical signals directly into sound waves. One of the simplest types of sound transducers is the piezo-ceramic loudspeaker. When you connect an alternating signal to the speaker the diaphragm oscillates at the same frequency as the input signal. As long as the oscillation frequency is within the human hearing range you will hear the signal.

The piezo-electric speaker has relatively high input impedance which means you can connect it directly to the Arduino output pins without loading the signal too much.

Illustration 22: Piezo mini loudspeaker

The following illustration shows how to wire up the speaker.

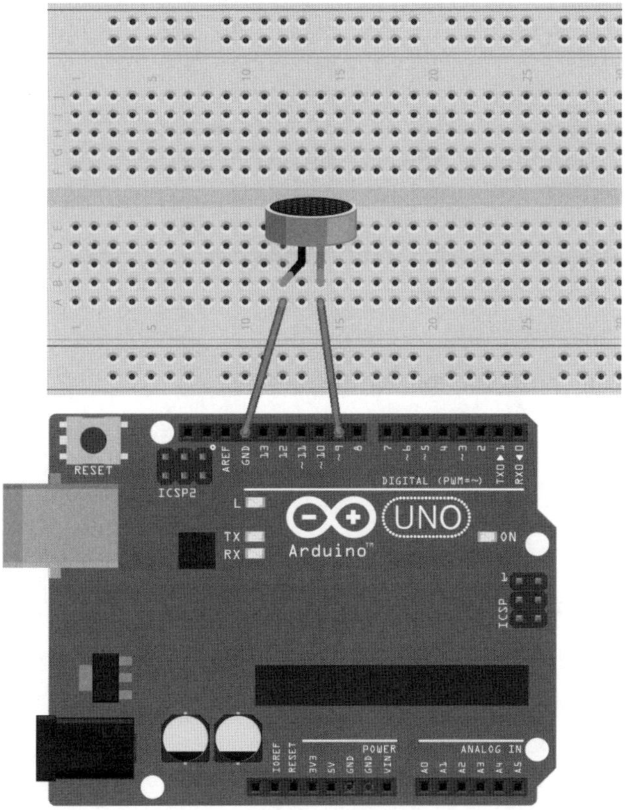

Illustration 23: The Arduino and piezo-speaker hook up

The PlayMelody.ino sketch plays a short sequence of notes on the speaker.

```
// PlayMelody.ino

int duration = 300, silence = 200;
int speakerPin=9;

// tone frequencies
int A =  440, H = 494;
int C =  523, d = 587, e =  659, f =  698;
int g =  784, a = 880, h =  988, c = 1047;

void setup()
{ pinMode(speakerPin, OUTPUT);
}

void loop()
{ tone(speakerPin,C,duration);  delay(silence);
  tone(speakerPin,d,duration);  delay(silence);
  tone(speakerPin,e,duration);  delay(silence);
  tone(speakerPin,f,duration);  delay(silence);
  tone(speakerPin,g,duration);  delay(silence);
  tone(speakerPin,e,duration);  delay(silence);
  tone(speakerPin,e,duration);  delay(silence);
  tone(speakerPin,f,duration);  delay(silence);
  tone(speakerPin,C,duration);  delay(silence);
  tone(speakerPin,C,duration);  delay(silence);
  delay(3*silence);
}
```

Load the program and press run to hear the melody.

The following program generates a piercing alarm signal.

```
// Alarm_signal.ino

int speakerPin=9;
int fstart = 100, fend = 2000;

void setup()
{ pinMode(speakerPin, OUTPUT);
}

void loop()
{ for(int i = fstart; i<= fend; i++)
  { tone(speakerPin,i,10);
  }
}
```

It's very easy to program a sound output signal. There are really no restrictions on simple sound sequences. With a little bit of imagination and patience you can produce quite impressive sounds.

2.7 Too few port pins? You need a shift register

The original Arduino Uno and its clones such as the SainSmart UNO have 14 digital I/O pins available for interfacing to the outside world. For most applications this number will be sufficient. For larger projects however it's usually not long before you begin to run out of free pins. In this case it's useful to be able to add some extra pins. A special IC can be used just for this purpose.

The SN74HC595N chip is an 8-bit shift register. It uses just three of the Arduino's I/O signals and provides 8 independent output signals. This chip is especially useful for driving devices like the 7-segment display or an 8x8 LED matrix.

When these eight I/Os are not enough it's easy to add more shift registers to give 16, 24 etc. without using any additional Arduino signals.

This chip contains two registers; the first is a shift register where the data as a serial stream is clocked through the eight register positions. The second register is the output register with all of its eight outputs connected to output pins. The data is sent as a serial stream, clocked through the shift register. When the stream of eight bits reaches the last position in the shift register a low-going 'LATCH' signal transfers the data in all of the eight register positions through to the output register where they now appear as outputs.

Illustration 24: The 74HC595 IC

Data moves along the shift register a bit like buckets of water being passed down a line to dowse a fire. When a new data bit is clocked into the first register position in the chain it passes its previous value to the next register and so on down the 8 register positions. Shifting is controlled by the signal on the CLOCK pin. At each clock edge data shifts one more position until after eight clock pulses the first bit of data is now in the eighth register position.

This exercise needs a slightly more complex hookup:

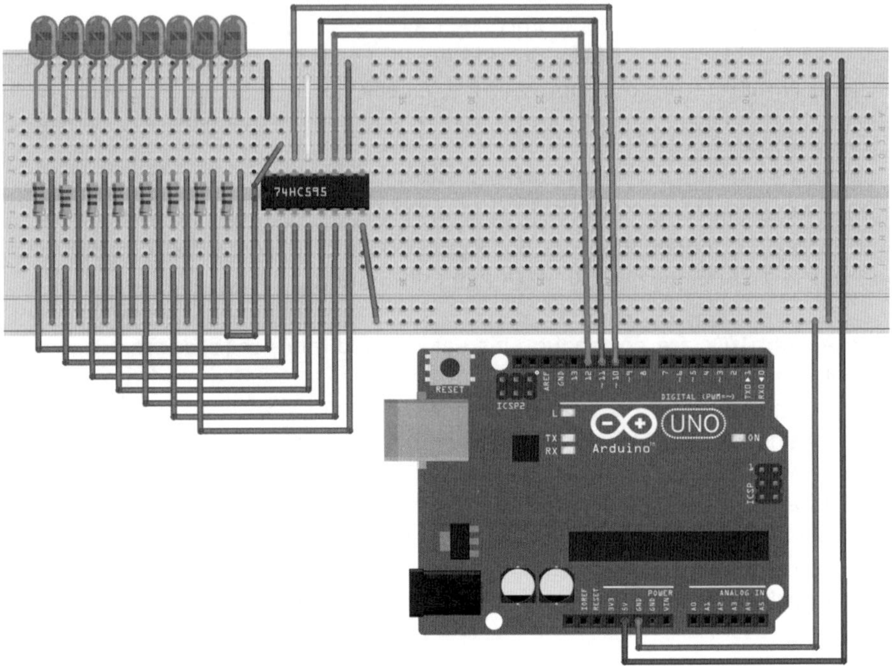

Illustration 25: Controlling 8 LEDs using the 74HC595

The following chapters describe a few practical applications using the shift register.

2.8 Binary counter

One interesting application using the shift register is the binary counter. The LEDs display the binary code for the number sequence from 0 to $2^8 - 1 = 255$. The first 32 binary values are given in the Table.

Decimal	**Bit 4**	**Bit 3**	**Bit 2**	**Bit 1**	**Bit 0**
0	0	0	0	0	0
1	0	0	0	0	1
2	0	0	0	1	0
3	0	0	0	1	1
4	0	0	1	0	0
5	0	0	1	0	1
6	0	0	1	1	0

7	0	0	1	1	1
8	0	1	0	0	0
9	0	1	0	0	1
10	0	1	0	1	0
11	0	1	0	1	1
12	0	1	1	0	0
13	0	1	1	0	1
14	0	1	1	1	0
15	0	1	1	1	1
16	1	0	0	0	0
17	1	0	0	0	1
18	1	0	0	1	0
19	1	0	0	1	1
20	1	0	1	0	0
21	1	0	1	0	1
22	1	0	1	1	0
23	1	0	1	1	1
24	1	1	0	0	0
25	1	1	0	0	1
26	1	1	0	1	0
27	1	1	0	1	1
28	1	1	1	0	0
29	1	1	1	0	1
30	1	1	1	1	0
31	1	1	1	1	1

Counting in binary values is very common in digital technology. You can also see examples of it in everyday life and there are even clocks in public places that show the time as a binary value.

The binary counter sketch looks like this:

```
// HC595_binary_counter.ino

int CLOCK = 12;
int LATCH = 11;
int DATA = 10;

int counter = 1;
```

```
void setup()
{ //set pins to output so you can control the shift register
  pinMode(LATCH, OUTPUT);
  pinMode(CLOCK, OUTPUT);
  pinMode(DATA, OUTPUT);
}

void loop()
{ digitalWrite(LATCH, LOW);
  shiftOut(DATA, CLOCK, MSBFIRST, counter);
  digitalWrite(LATCH, HIGH);
  delay(100);
  counter++;
  if (counter >= 256) counter=1;
}
```

When you start the program running the LEDs display binary values starting from 0 and going up to 255. It's a good opportunity to get more acquainted with the sequence.

2.9 Model airfield runway lights

It is also easy to change the sequence in which the string of 8 LEDs is switched so that instead of a binary counter value it displays a running light or chaser effect. All we need to change is one line in the sketch. Instead of

```
counter++;
```

replace it with

```
counter*=2;
```

Now the counter value isn't increment by 1 each time but by powers of two. It now only contains values of 2^n which results in just a single LED lit at each count, effectively moving along the LEDs to give a chaser effect.

Practical applications of this effect can, for example be found in the world of model building. It could be used to simulate runway landing lights for a model helicopter or quadcopter. This would make an effective landing pad in a darkened living room. Model car race tracks or even train layouts would also benefit from the lighting effect.

The sketch to make this chaser light is under HC595_chaser.ino in the download pack for this book.

2.10 Serial Data Output

As well as showing binary count values and chaser effects you can also write different sequences into the shift register to produce other lighting patterns. This sketch generates

a lighting effect where LEDs 1, 3, 5, and 7 are all lit together alternating with LEDs 2, 4, 6 and 8.
You can experiment with different patterns and different delay times to create the most diverse lighting effects.

This sketch alternates the lighting using two patterns.

```
int dataA[8] = {1,0,1,0,1,0,1,0};
int dataB[8] = {0,1,0,1,0,1,0,1};
```

After the pin assignments have been declared the patterns are shifted into the register:

```
  for (int i=0; i<8; i++)
  { digitalWrite(CLOCK, LOW);
    digitalWrite(DATA, dataA[i]);
    digitalWrite(CLOCK, HIGH);
```

The clock signal is driven low before then high after each new data value is output. After eight bits are output the LATCH signal shifts this eight-bit value into the output register:

```
  digitalWrite(LATCH, HIGH);
```

The complete sketch looks like this:

```
// HC595_shift_out.ino

int CLOCK = 12;
int LATCH = 11;
int DATA = 10;

int dataA[8] = {1,0,1,0,1,0,1,0};
int dataB[8] = {0,1,0,1,0,1,0,1};

void setup()
{ pinMode(LATCH, OUTPUT);
  pinMode(CLOCK, OUTPUT);
  pinMode(DATA, OUTPUT);
}

void loop ()
{ digitalWrite(LATCH, LOW);
  for (int i=0; i<8; i++)
  { digitalWrite(CLOCK, LOW);
    digitalWrite(DATA, dataA[i]);
    digitalWrite(CLOCK, HIGH);
  }
```

```
        digitalWrite(LATCH, HIGH);
        delay(300);

        digitalWrite(LATCH, LOW);
        for (int i=0; i<8; i++)
        { digitalWrite(CLOCK, LOW);
          digitalWrite(DATA, dataB[i]);
          digitalWrite(CLOCK, HIGH);
        }
        digitalWrite(LATCH, HIGH);
        delay(300);
      }
```

Illustration 26: Serial Data Output

2.11 Voltage measurement on a row of LEDs

In this application we use the same row of eight LEDs from the previous example, this time one of the eight LEDs is lit to indicate the level of the measured analog voltage. We make use of a new component called a potentiometer or 'pot' in this experiment to generate the variable voltage.

Illustration 27: A Potentiometer or pot

Here's how you hookup the pot to the Arduino while using the same row of LEDs to output the measured voltage level. Turning the pot changes the measured input voltage level and this is indicated by which of the eight LEDs is lit. The measured analog values are also output to the serial monitor.

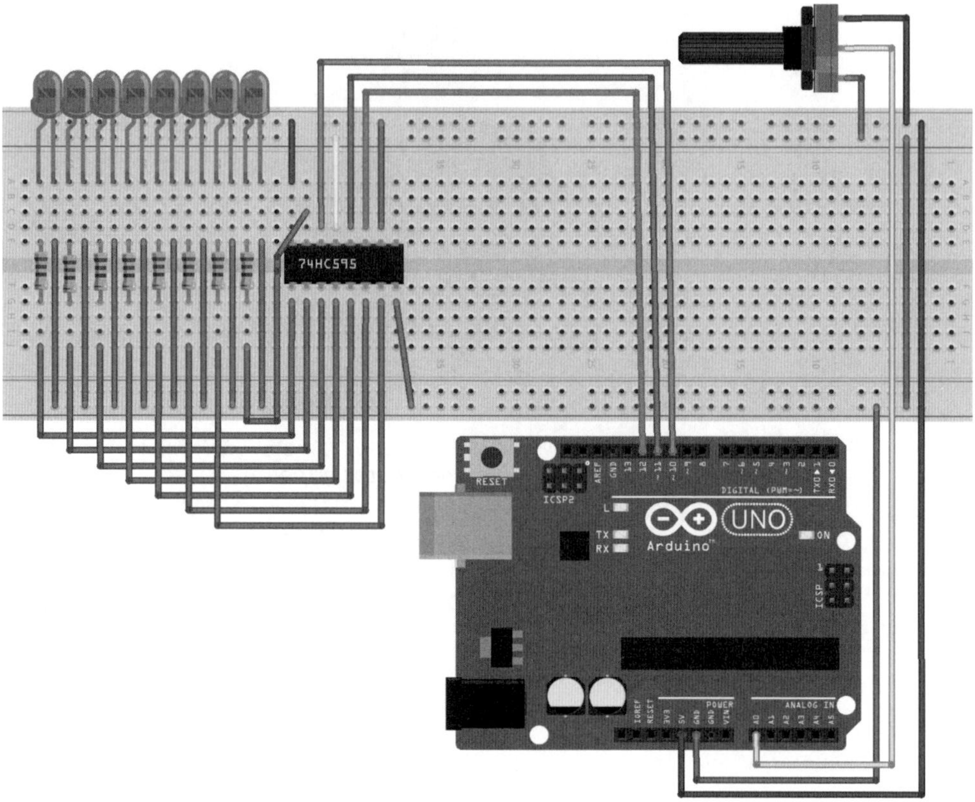

Illustration 28: Voltage measurement with LED level indicator

The sketch for this one looks like this:

```
// HC595_poti_voltmeter.ino

int CLOCK = 12;
int LATCH = 11;
int DATA = 10;
const int analogInPin = A0;
const int analogOutPin = 9;
int sensorValue = 0, mappedValue = 0, outputValue = 0;

void setup()
{ pinMode(LATCH, OUTPUT);
  pinMode(CLOCK, OUTPUT);
  pinMode(DATA, OUTPUT);
  Serial.begin(9600);
}

void loop()
```

```
{ sensorValue = analogRead(analogInPin);
  mappedValue = map(sensorValue, 0, 1050, 0, 8);
  outputValue = (1 << mappedValue);
  Serial.print("sensor = ");
  Serial.print(sensorValue);
  Serial.print("\t mapped = ");
  Serial.print(mappedValue);
  Serial.print("\t output = ");
  Serial.println(outputValue);

  digitalWrite(LATCH, LOW);
  shiftOut(DATA, CLOCK, MSBFIRST, outputValue);
  digitalWrite(LATCH, HIGH);
  delay(100);
}
```

Chapter 3 • Display Technology

Displays are in the widest sense the interface between man and machine. Together with input devices such as pushbuttons switches and keyboards output devices are also practically indispensible to the operation of electronic systems. At its most basic a simple LED can be used to indicate a condition. It can be used to indicate a particular operating mode of a device or to alert an operator that some limit value has been exceeded, a bright red LED, for example is an effective indicator of an over-temperature condition.

When you need to indicate additional information more complex displays will be necessary. The Liquid Crystal Display (LCD) is a very popular form of display technology. They can be used to show digital values and use characters to convey easily readable messages.

3.1 An LCD for the Arduino

An LCD can be used as a universal output device for the Arduino. The display included in the kit has the following properties:

- It communicates via an I^2C-Bus – Address range: 0x20 to 0x27 (0x20 is the default)
- White characters on a blue background
- Operating voltage: 5V
- Contrast adjustable using a pot
- Display size: 82 mm x 35 mm x 18 mm

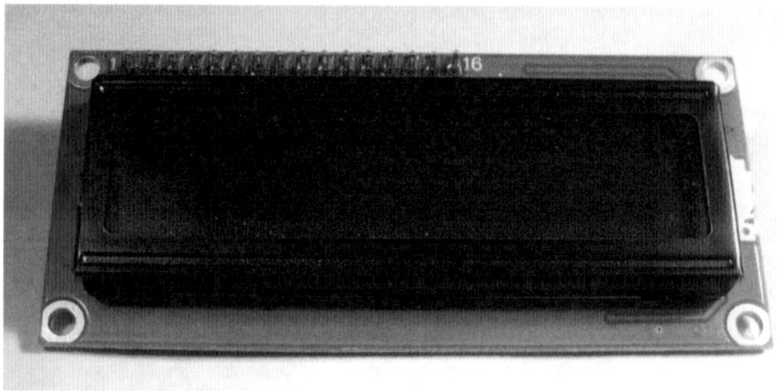

Illustration 29: LCD module

Without doubt LCDs are amongst the most important peripheral components used with microcontroller-based systems. They can display numbers, letters and also various special characters. They will also give your projects a more profession look. The values of temperature, voltage levels and other measurements can be represented accurately on the display as well as more mundane things such as time of day and text messages.

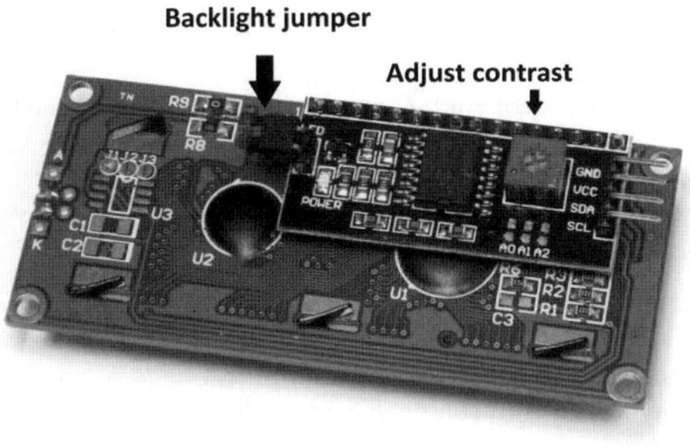

Illustration 30: The LCD module from the back

In contrast to LED dot-matrix displays LCDs are almost exclusively supplied with an integrated controller chip. This is because the dot-matrix LCD has a very large number of pixels needing to be controlled. Even a relatively small 2-line 16 character display is made up of over 1000 pixels. This would far exceed the resources available from an AVR microcontroller. These LCDs therefore form part of a display module with an integrated controller chip. One of the most popular types of controller chips is the HD44780. These can be controlled with just 16 connections. A close look at the display module will reveal the single row of 16 pin header type connections along the top edge of the board.

Connecting all 16 of these pins to the Arduino would use up a lot of the Arduino's I/O capability. There are methods of using the display module which reduce the number of connections required but we would still need at least six I/O pins.

Besides the large display controller chip on the display module there is also a smaller chip which provides the module with an I^2C serial interface so the number of I/O pins required is now reduced to just two for controlling the display. This is an important advantage especially for larger more complex projects which use a large number of Arduino pins. Another difference compared with the standard LCD module is that this one includes a pot to control the display contrast.

If you can't see any characters on the display when you start using it, try twiddling the contrast control pot using a small screwdriver pushed into the central slot in the pot to find the optimal setting.

With the serial interface cabling between the Arduino and display module is now down to just four wires. GND connects to the GND pin on the microcontroller and Vcc with the 5V Pin on the Arduino or Sainsmart Uno board.

The connection labeled SDA on the display module connects to the Uno analog input A4 and SCL to analog input A5. These pins have a double function; they can be used with analog input signals and also to provide the I²C-Interface signals. The table below shows the four wire hookup between the Arduino and the LCD display module:

LCD module pin	Description	Arduino pin	Arduino function
Vcc	Supply voltage	5 V	
GND	Ground	GND	
SDA	Serial Data	A4	SDA
SCL	Serial Clock	A5	SCL

To use the LCD module with the I²C interface you will need a library which is not pre-installed in the Arduino-IDE. You can download the library from

https://github.com/fdebrabander/Arduino-LiquidCrystal-I2C-library

and install it in the Arduino IDE.

The following illustration shows how to connect the module to the Arduino:

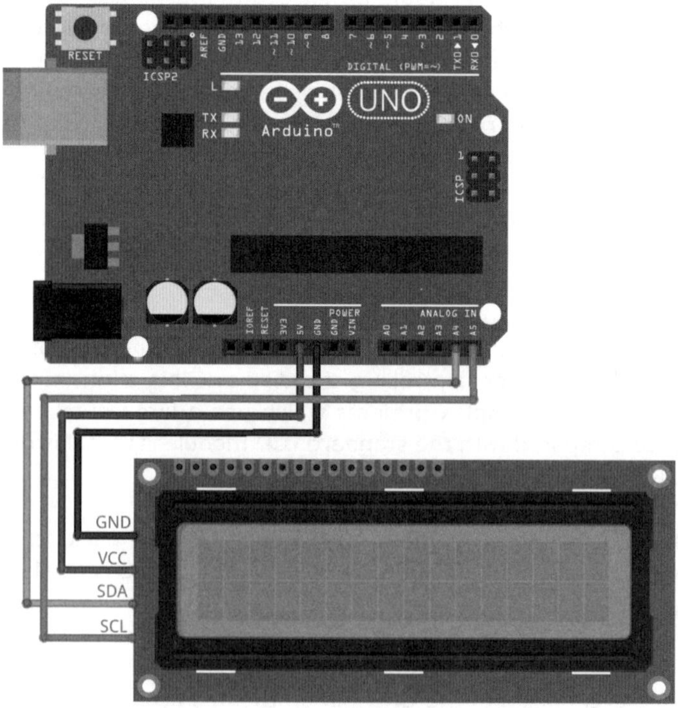

Illustration 31: I2C LCD with the Arduino

To check that the display is correctly connected you can load and run this sketch:

```
// I2C_LCD_test.ino

#include <Wire.h>
#include <LiquidCrystal_I2C.h>

// Set the LCD address to 0x27 for a 16 chars and 2 line display
LiquidCrystal_I2C lcd(0x27, 16, 2);

void setup()
{ // initialize the LCD
  lcd.init();
  // Turn on the blacklight and print a message.
  lcd.backlight();
  lcd.print("LCD ok!");
}

void loop()
{
}
```

An LCD is best suited to display sensor values such as temperature or brightness values. Voltage levels at the analog ports or level states of the digital inputs can also be easily displayed.

3.2 Attention! Warning Signal Display

The LCD module allows you to control its backlight brightness using software commands via the I²C interface.
We could use a light sensor to measure the light level and automatically adjust the back-light brightness accordingly or turn the backlight on or off as required.

Another possibility is to make the displayed message flash on and off. This allows us to clearly show warning messages. The following sketch flashes the message 'ALERT' several times a second as an example warning message. This type of displayed message is particularly useful for providing readings from a sensor. A system to measure engine temperature, for example could display the temperature value continously while it's within acceptable limits. As soon as the upper level is exceeded the value can flash to warn of an engine overheat event.

```
// LCD_blinking.ino

#include <Wire.h>
#include <LiquidCrystal_I2C.h>
LiquidCrystal_I2C lcd(0x27,16,2);  // set the LCD address to 0x27 for a 16
chars and 2 line display
```

```
void setup()
{ lcd.init();       //initialize LCD
  lcd.print("      ALERT!      ");

}
void loop()
{ lcd.backlight();  // backlight on
  delay(200);
  lcd.noBacklight();  // backlight off
  delay(200);
}
```

The display is very versatile and will also be used for several other projects in the book. There is a humidity/temperature sensor project and also a clock with battery-backup.

3.3 Driving Seven-Segment Displays

Digits can be displayed simply and efficiently with so-called seven-segment displays. Such displays actually often consist of eight LED elements (seven segments plus a decimal point). The LED segments are arranged in the shape of an eight. By switching certain segments on, the digits from 0 to 9 can be displayed in a clearly legible form.

As well as numbers, some capital letters can also be displayed (eg A, C, E, F, etc.). If you want to display additional letters, you can use a type of display with sixteen segments. These are however not so common and therefore expensive.

Seven-segment displays are produced in a wide variety of sizes, colors, and terminal configurations. A widely used type is shown in the following illustration. The individual segments are usually designated with the letters **a** through to **g**. The LEDs in each of the segments share a common connection; they are either designated as common anode (CA) or common cathode (CC) types.

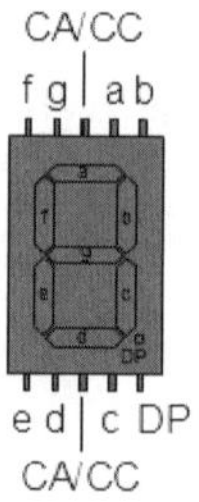

Illustration 32: The segment designations

Illustration 33: An LED seven-segment display

Even with just a single seven-segment display it's possible to indicate many things. It can display the operating status of some equipment or machine. A washing machine, for example often has one on the front panel indicating what stage of the wash cycle it's at. Telephone answer machines often use one to indicate the number of calls received and motorbikes use them to indicate gear selection.

The main technical characteristics of the 5161AS seven segment display:

- LED color: red,
- 1 position
- 20mA per segment (approx)
- Common Cathode (CC)

The next illustration following shows the connections between the 7-segment display and the Uno. The photo beneath shows the display plugged in to the prototyping breadboard, the series-connected resistors are also shown.

You can choose values of either 220 Ohm or 1 KOhm- depending on the display brightness you want.

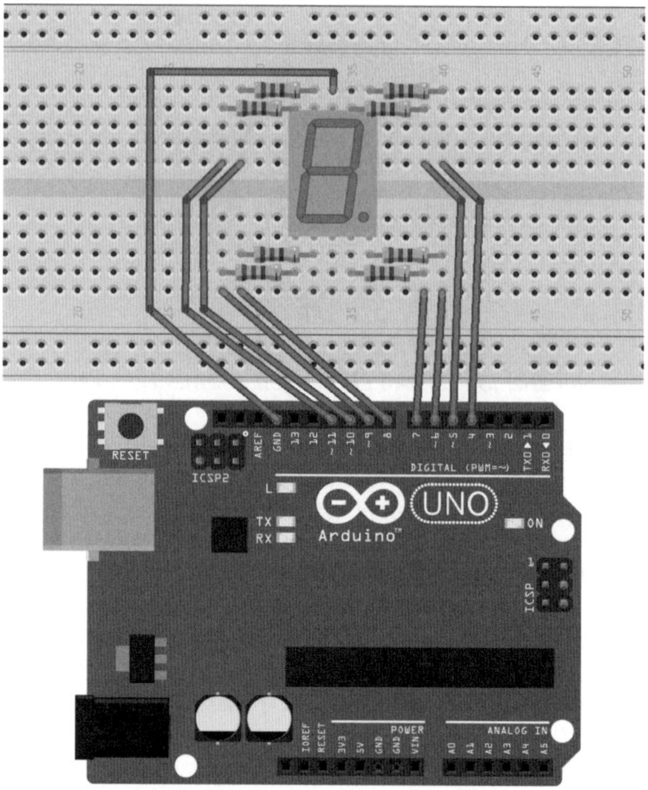

Illustration 34: Wiring the 7-segment display on the breadboard

Illustration 35: The display in action!

A simple sketch to control the display:

```
// Seven-Segment_single.ino

const int a=4;  const int b=5;
const int dp=6; const int c=7;
const int d=8;  const int e=9;
const int f=10; const int g=11;

int timeDelay = 300;

void setup()
{ for(int thisPin = 4; thisPin <= 11; thisPin++)
  { pinMode(thisPin,OUTPUT);
  }
}

void loop()
{ digital_0();  delay(timeDelay);
  digital_1();  delay(timeDelay);
  digital_2();  delay(timeDelay);
  digital_3();  delay(timeDelay);
  digital_4();  delay(timeDelay);
  digital_5();  delay(timeDelay);
  digital_6();  delay(timeDelay);
  digital_7();  delay(timeDelay);
  digital_8();  delay(timeDelay);
  digital_9();  delay(timeDelay);
}

void digital_0(void) // zero
{ digitalWrite(a,HIGH);  digitalWrite(b,HIGH);
  digitalWrite(c,HIGH);  digitalWrite(d,HIGH);
  digitalWrite(e,HIGH);  digitalWrite(f,HIGH);
  digitalWrite(g,LOW);  digitalWrite(dp,LOW);
}
void digital_1(void) // one
{ digitalWrite(a,LOW);  digitalWrite(b,HIGH);
  digitalWrite(c,HIGH);  digitalWrite(d,LOW);
  digitalWrite(e,LOW);  digitalWrite(f,LOW);
  digitalWrite(g,LOW);  digitalWrite(dp,LOW);
}
void digital_2(void) // two
{ digitalWrite(a,HIGH);  digitalWrite(b,HIGH);
  digitalWrite(c,LOW);  digitalWrite(d,HIGH);
  digitalWrite(e,HIGH);  digitalWrite(f,LOW);
```

```
  digitalWrite(g,HIGH);  digitalWrite(dp,LOW);
}
void digital_3(void) // three
{ digitalWrite(a,HIGH);  digitalWrite(b,HIGH);
  digitalWrite(c,HIGH);  digitalWrite(d,HIGH);
  digitalWrite(e,LOW);  digitalWrite(f,LOW);
  digitalWrite(g,HIGH);  digitalWrite(dp,LOW);
}
void digital_4(void) // four
{ digitalWrite(a,LOW);  digitalWrite(b,HIGH);
  digitalWrite(c,HIGH);  digitalWrite(d,LOW);
  digitalWrite(e,LOW);  digitalWrite(f,HIGH);
  digitalWrite(g,HIGH);  digitalWrite(dp,LOW);
}
void digital_5(void) // five
{ digitalWrite(a,HIGH);  digitalWrite(b,LOW);
  digitalWrite(c,HIGH);  digitalWrite(d,HIGH);
  digitalWrite(e,LOW);  digitalWrite(f,HIGH);
  digitalWrite(g,HIGH);  digitalWrite(dp,LOW);
}
void digital_6(void) // six
{ digitalWrite(a,HIGH);  digitalWrite(b,LOW);
  digitalWrite(c,HIGH);  digitalWrite(d,HIGH);
  digitalWrite(e,HIGH);  digitalWrite(f,HIGH);
  digitalWrite(g,HIGH);  digitalWrite(dp,LOW);
}
void digital_7(void) // seven
{ digitalWrite(a,HIGH);  digitalWrite(b,HIGH);
  digitalWrite(c,HIGH);  digitalWrite(d,LOW);
  digitalWrite(e,LOW);  digitalWrite(f,LOW);
  digitalWrite(g,LOW);  digitalWrite(dp,LOW);
}
void digital_8(void) // eight
{ digitalWrite(a,HIGH);  digitalWrite(b,HIGH);
  digitalWrite(c,HIGH);  digitalWrite(d,HIGH);
  digitalWrite(e,HIGH);  digitalWrite(f,HIGH);
  digitalWrite(g,HIGH);  digitalWrite(dp,LOW);
}
void digital_9(void) // nine
{ digitalWrite(a,HIGH);  digitalWrite(b,HIGH);
  digitalWrite(c,HIGH);  digitalWrite(d,HIGH);
  digitalWrite(e,LOW);  digitalWrite(f,HIGH);
  digitalWrite(g,HIGH);  digitalWrite(dp,LOW);
}
```

In this part of the program each segment of the display is assigned an Arduino pin number.

```
const int a=4;  const int b=5;
const int dp=6; const int c=7;
const int d=8;  const int e=9;
const int f=10; const int g=11;
```

They are configured as outputs in the Setup.

The digits are controlled by a separate subroutine. For example to display a 'zero' all segments except **g** light up. All other outputs must therefore be set to HIGH, only the **g** and the decimal point (dp) are written to with a LOW signal:

```
void digital_0(void) // zero
{ digitalWrite(a,HIGH);  digitalWrite(b,HIGH);
  digitalWrite(c,HIGH);  digitalWrite(d,HIGH);
  digitalWrite(e,HIGH);  digitalWrite(f,HIGH);
  digitalWrite(g,LOW);  digitalWrite(dp,LOW);
```

All the other numbers are generated in the same way. In the main loop, all numbers are displayed one after the other.

3.4 Pin-saving Shift Register

A disadvantage of the method used in the last project to drive the 7-segment LED is that it uses up seven (or eight if you want the decimal point) pins of the Arduino. On larger projects you will quickly run out of pins because you will be using some pins to perform other functions. We already looked in an earlier chapter at how we can save pins by using a shift register. We can also use the same strategy here with an HC595 shift register chip to drive the LED.

Although the wiring layout on the breadboard looks a bit complicated there are only three wires required to drive data and control the 7-segment LED. Power must also be supplied to the breadboard from the Arduino connectors.

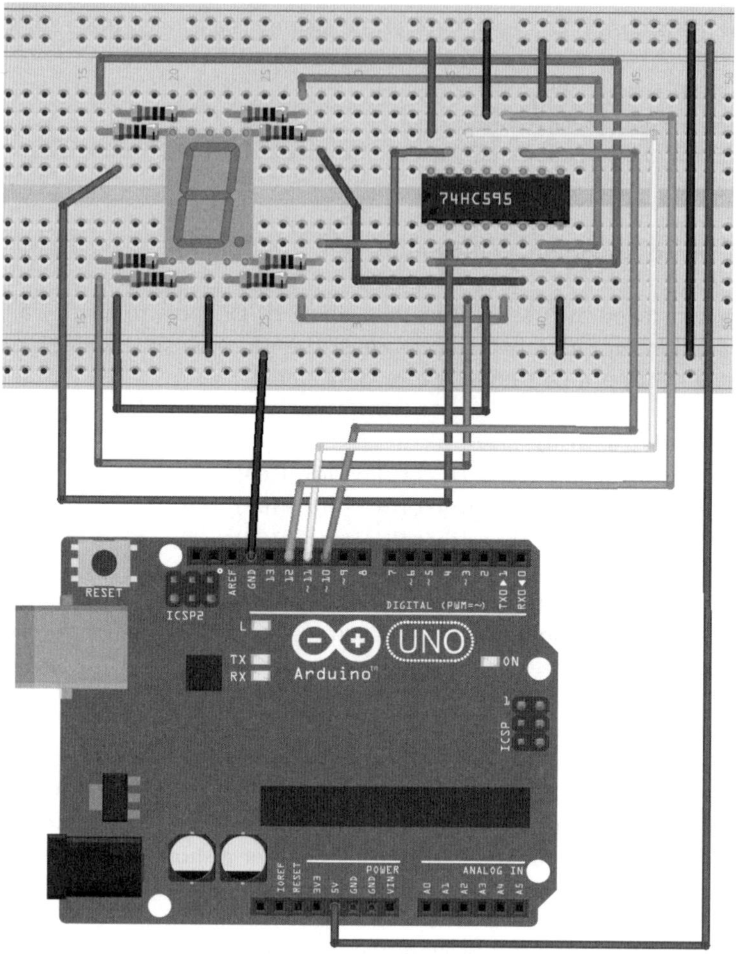

Illustration 36: Driving a display with a shift register

There are a relatively large number of wires needed, check the following table to make it easier it shows the connections from the HC595 to the seven-segment display. It's easier if you progress one cable at a time, plugging the ends into their correct positions.

IC pin	1	2	3	4	5	6	7	15
Display-Segment	f	g	e	d	c	b	a	DP

The sketch to control the display is given here:

```
// HC595_seven-segment.ino

const int latchPin = 11;//Pin connected to ST_CP of 74HC595
const int clockPin = 12;//Pin connected to SH_CP of 74HC595
```

```
const int dataPin = 10; //Pin connected to DS of 74HC595

// display 0,1,2,3,4,5,6,7,8,9,A,b,C,d,E,F

int datArray[16] = {252, 96, 218, 242, 102, 182, 190, 224, 254, 246, 238,
62, 156, 122, 158, 142};

void setup ()
{ pinMode(latchPin,OUTPUT);
  pinMode(clockPin,OUTPUT);
  pinMode(dataPin,OUTPUT);
}

void loop()
{ for(int num = 0; num < 16; num++)
  { digitalWrite(latchPin,LOW);
    shiftOut(dataPin,clockPin,MSBFIRST,datArray[num]);
    digitalWrite(latchPin,HIGH); //set latch to save data
    delay(1000);
  }
}
```

Each displayed character is encoded as a number in an array. The number results from the binary code required to light the corresponding segments on the 7-segment display. The codes are transferred to the shift register as described in chapter 2.8.

The difference is now that the eight LEDs are arranged into the shape of a number 8 with the decimal point at the lower right corner rather than all in a line in chapter 2.8.

3.5 Universally useful: The 4x7 segment Display Module

As we've seen already a single 7-segment digit is useful for lots of applications, it's just about right for showing things such as washing machine program cycle stage and motorbike gear number selection.

However, if there is more information to display such as the value of a measurement or the time of day, you will really need a display with more digits. A four-digit display is quite versatile. If the digits also have decimal point display or a colon then you can use it as a display for a digital voltmeter or clock.

The 4 x 7-segment LED display included in the kit lights up with red segments, the maximum current for each segment is 20 mA. All the LEDs in each of the four positions of this display share a common cathode connection. A suitable type is the 5461AS or compatible.

The following illustration shows the corresponding pin layout:

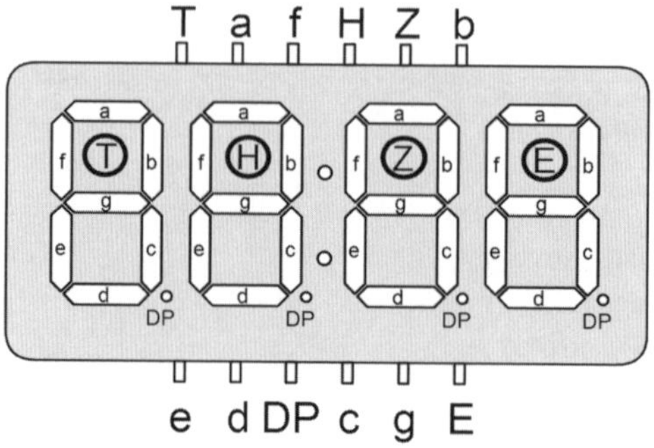

Illustration 37: Pin layout of the 4-character display

Illustration 38: 4x7 segment LED display

This display has good legibility in most lighting conditions:

Illustration 39: Numbers on the 4 x 7- segment LED display

Here's how we can connect it to the Arduino using a breadboard.

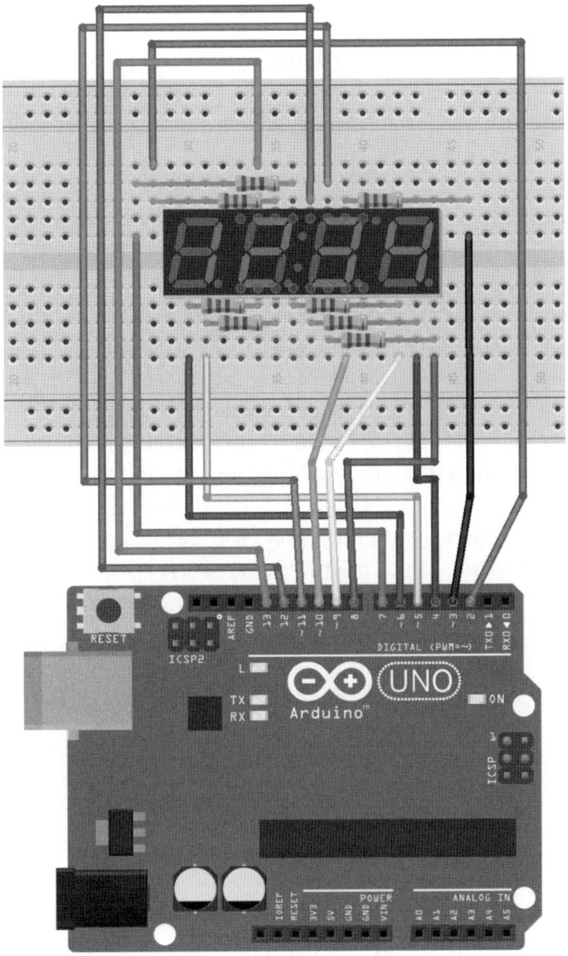

Illustration 40: Wiring the 4x7-segment LED display

3.6 A Counter... Not just for beans

The first exercise we will do with the 7-segment display is to build a simple counter. For this you will need to load the 'counter.ino' sketch to the Arduino.

This sketch just counts from 0000 to 9999 and shows the value on the display.

```
// Seven-segment_counter.ino

#include <TimerOne.h>

// pin connection - segments
int seg_a = 2;  int seg_b = 3; int seg_c = 4;  int seg_d = 5;
int seg_e = 6;  int seg_f = 7; int seg_g = 8;  int seg_dp = 9;
```

```
// pin connection - digits
int dig_1 = 13; int dig_2 = 12; int dig_3 = 11; int dig_4 = 10;

// display value: 0000 to 9999, digit-number: 1 to 4, counter variable
int number = 0, digit = 0, count = 0;

int timetune = 1;    // fine tuning of display timing

void setup()
{ pinMode(dig_1, OUTPUT); pinMode(dig_2, OUTPUT);
  pinMode(dig_3, OUTPUT); pinMode(dig_4, OUTPUT);
  pinMode(seg_a, OUTPUT); pinMode(seg_b, OUTPUT);
  pinMode(seg_c, OUTPUT); pinMode(seg_d, OUTPUT);
  pinMode(seg_e, OUTPUT); pinMode(seg_f, OUTPUT);
  pinMode(seg_g, OUTPUT); pinMode(seg_dp, OUTPUT);

  Timer1.initialize(10000); // timer for 10000 µs = 10 ms = .01 s
  Timer1.attachInterrupt( countUp ); // attach service routine countUp
}

void loop()
{ clrDigit();  Digit(0);  Number((number/1000));  delay(timetune);
  clrDigit();  Digit(1);  Number((number%1000)/100);  delay(timetune);
  clrDigit();  Digit(2);  Number(number%100/10);  delay(timetune);
  clrDigit();  Digit(3);  Number(number%10);  delay(timetune);
}
/*************************************/
void Digit(int digit)
{ digitalWrite(dig_1, HIGH);  digitalWrite(dig_2, HIGH);
  digitalWrite(dig_3, HIGH);  digitalWrite(dig_4, HIGH);

  switch(digit)
  { case 0: digitalWrite(dig_1, LOW);  break;
    case 1: digitalWrite(dig_2, LOW);  break;
    case 2: digitalWrite(dig_3, LOW);  break;
    case 3: digitalWrite(dig_4, LOW);  break;
  }
}

//display numbers
void Number(int digit)
{ switch(digit)
  { default:    zero();    break;
    case 1:     one();     break;
    case 2:     two();     break;
    case 3:     three();   break;
```

```
      case 4:     four();     break;
      case 5:     five();     break;
      case 6:     six();      break;
      case 7:     seven();    break;
      case 8:     eight();    break;
      case 9:     nine();     break;
    }
  }

  void clrDigit()
  { digitalWrite(seg_a, LOW);  digitalWrite(seg_b, LOW);
    digitalWrite(seg_c, LOW);  digitalWrite(seg_d, LOW);
    digitalWrite(seg_e, LOW);  digitalWrite(seg_f, LOW);
    digitalWrite(seg_g, LOW);  digitalWrite(seg_dp, LOW);
  }
  void zero() // 0
  { digitalWrite(seg_a, HIGH);  digitalWrite(seg_b, HIGH);
    digitalWrite(seg_c, HIGH);  digitalWrite(seg_d, HIGH);
    digitalWrite(seg_e, HIGH);  digitalWrite(seg_f, HIGH);
    digitalWrite(seg_g, LOW);
  }
  void one()  // 1
  { digitalWrite(seg_a, LOW);  digitalWrite(seg_b, HIGH);
    digitalWrite(seg_c, HIGH); digitalWrite(seg_d, LOW);
    digitalWrite(seg_e, LOW);  digitalWrite(seg_f, LOW);
    digitalWrite(seg_g, LOW);
  }
  void two()  // 2
  { digitalWrite(seg_a, HIGH);  digitalWrite(seg_b, HIGH);
    digitalWrite(seg_c, LOW);   digitalWrite(seg_d, HIGH);
    digitalWrite(seg_e, HIGH);  digitalWrite(seg_f, LOW);
    digitalWrite(seg_g, HIGH);
  }
  void three()  // 3
  { digitalWrite(seg_a, HIGH);  digitalWrite(seg_b, HIGH);
    digitalWrite(seg_c, HIGH);  digitalWrite(seg_d, HIGH);
    digitalWrite(seg_e, LOW);   digitalWrite(seg_f, LOW);
    digitalWrite(seg_g, HIGH);
  }
  void four()  // 4
  { digitalWrite(seg_a, LOW);  digitalWrite(seg_b, HIGH);
    digitalWrite(seg_c, HIGH); digitalWrite(seg_d, LOW);
    digitalWrite(seg_e, LOW);  digitalWrite(seg_f, HIGH);
    digitalWrite(seg_g, HIGH);
  }
  void five()  // 5
```

```
{ digitalWrite(seg_a, HIGH);  digitalWrite(seg_b, LOW);
  digitalWrite(seg_c, HIGH);  digitalWrite(seg_d, HIGH);
  digitalWrite(seg_e, LOW);   digitalWrite(seg_f, HIGH);
  digitalWrite(seg_g, HIGH);
}
void six()  // 6
{ digitalWrite(seg_a, HIGH);  digitalWrite(seg_b, LOW);
  digitalWrite(seg_c, HIGH);  digitalWrite(seg_d, HIGH);
  digitalWrite(seg_e, HIGH);  digitalWrite(seg_f, HIGH);
  digitalWrite(seg_g, HIGH);
}

void seven()  // 7
{ digitalWrite(seg_a, HIGH);  digitalWrite(seg_b, HIGH);
  digitalWrite(seg_c, HIGH);  digitalWrite(seg_d, LOW);
  digitalWrite(seg_e, LOW);   digitalWrite(seg_f, LOW);
  digitalWrite(seg_g, LOW);
}
void eight()  // 8
{ digitalWrite(seg_a, HIGH);  digitalWrite(seg_b, HIGH);
  digitalWrite(seg_c, HIGH);  digitalWrite(seg_d, HIGH);
  digitalWrite(seg_e, HIGH);  digitalWrite(seg_f, HIGH);
  digitalWrite(seg_g, HIGH);
}
void nine()  // 9
{ digitalWrite(seg_a, HIGH);  digitalWrite(seg_b, HIGH);
  digitalWrite(seg_c, HIGH);  digitalWrite(seg_d, HIGH);
  digitalWrite(seg_e, LOW);   digitalWrite(seg_f, HIGH);
  digitalWrite(seg_g, HIGH);
}

void countUp()
{   count ++;
    if(count == 10)
    { count = 0;
      number ++; if(number == 10000)  number = 0;
    }
}
```

The sketch is similar to the program earlier for the single display unit. Again each digit is defined in its own subroutine.

With the need to drive four characters the display routine will be slightly more complicated. For this display we make use of a technique called multiplexing. This technique means that there is only ever one of the four displayed characters on at any instant. One character after another is switched on in the appropriate pattern which represents the number displayed. When the switching speed between each character is fast enough your eye will not be able to detect any display flicker.

The program to perform this simple counting task is quite long and complex. For more ambitious projects there are various library functions that will help simplify the necessary sketch writing process.

This cuts down on the programming effort and helps you focus on the actual application.

3.7 The SevenSeg Library

In the last chapter we showed the nuts and bolts of how the 4 x 7 segment display can be driven, now we make use of some library routines which can be downloaded free of charge from

http://sim.marebakken.com/SevenSeg.zip

Using the routines contained in this library makes it a cinch to show symbols and numbers on the display as can be seen from the following sketch.

```
// Seven_segment_number_display.ino

#include <SevenSeg.h>

// segments              a  b  c  d  e  f   g
SevenSeg disp        (2 ,3 ,4 ,5 ,6 ,7 ,8);

const int numOfDigits = 4;

// Arduino pins              D10  D11  D12   D13
// digit                          4     2      2       1
int digitPins [numOfDigits]={  13,  12,  11,   10};
char str[4];

void setup ()
{ disp.setCommonCathode();
  disp.setDigitPins (numOfDigits, digitPins);

}

void loop ()
{ disp.write("1234");
}
```

Now we only need to assign the segments and the digit position in the sketch to the I/O pins, the rest of the work is taken care of by the library routines.
To save rewiring we have just used the same segment assignments from the previous sketch shown in illustration 3.13.

3.8 A Digital Clock

With the help of library routines we can make a digital clock in no time. First you need to get and load the 'Time' library to the Arduino IDE.
This can be found here:

https://github.com/PaulStoffregen/Time

```
// Digital_clock.ino

#include <Time.h>
#include <SevenSeg.h>

// segments          a  b  c  d  e  f  g
SevenSeg disp       (2 ,3 ,4 ,5 ,6 ,7 ,8);

const int numOfDigits=4;
// Arduino pins                 D10  D11  D12   D13
// digit                        4    2    2     1
int digitPins [numOfDigits]={  13,  12,  11,   10};

void setup()
{ // 20:15:00 am 1. Januar 2017.
  setTime(20, 15, 00, 01, 01, 2017);
  disp.setCommonCathode();
  disp.setDigitPins (numOfDigits, digitPins);
  disp.setDPPin(9); // pin for decimal dot
}

void loop()
{  if ((second()%2) == 0) disp.writeClock(hour(), minute(), '.');
   if ((second()%2) == 1) disp.writeClock(hour(), minute(), '_');
}
```

This is a stark example of how library routines simplify the process of sketch writing. If you decided to write the sketch from scratch without using any library routines you would probably be looking at over 100 lines and many hours at the keyboard. With the help of suitable libraries however the job is done with just a few lines of code.

3.9 For Numbers, Characters and Icons: 8x8 Dot Matrix Display

Seven-segment displays are ideal for displaying numbers and a limited range of characters. Some letters such as the A, the C, or even an E are shown quite well but 7-segment displays for text output are not really optimal. Letters such as W or V cannot be represented. Alternatively, dot-matrix displays are much better suited for this. Even simple icons or small graphics can be displayed.
For this project an 8 x 8 LED dot matrix with 64 LEDs in total is used. The SH1388ASR dot matrix display is a suitable device and uses red LEDs. The current consumption of a single

LED is approximately 15 mA. All the LEDs in each row have a common cathode connection. Pin 1 is identified where the lead exits the package.

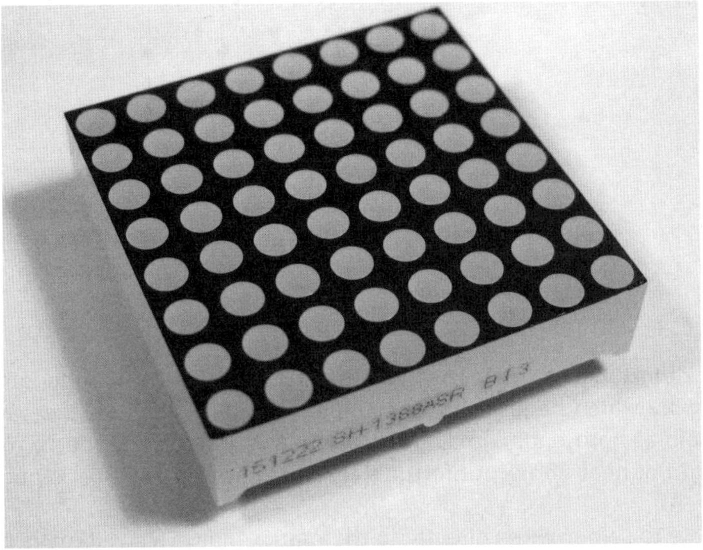

Illustration 41: LED Dot-Matrix module

To control each of the 64 LEDs in the 8 x 8 dot matrix display we could have a connection to the anode of each LED and use one common cathode. This would result in a total of 65 connections altogether. Much less wiring is involved if the LEDs are connected as a matrix. Here in the matrix eight LEDs share a common column connection and eight connections provide the row selection. Instead of 65 connections which we would need if each LED were wired individually, we only need 8 + 8 = 16 connections.

The way in which individual LEDs are selected in a matrix is shown in the following illustration. For simplicity a 3 x 4 matrix is used to illustrate the principle. Instead of 13 connections necessary to address each LED individually the matrix arrangement cuts this down to just 7.

For example to turn on the 2nd LED in the 2nd row it is necessary to put a HIGH on the anodes of all the LEDs in that column and then put a LOW on the second row which connects to the cathodes of all the LEDs in that row. In this state there will only be one LED which has the correct conditions for current to flow. Changing the states of the row and column drive signals allows you to address any LED in the matrix.

The following diagram shows how the LEDs are wired up in the matrix display and how one can be selected:

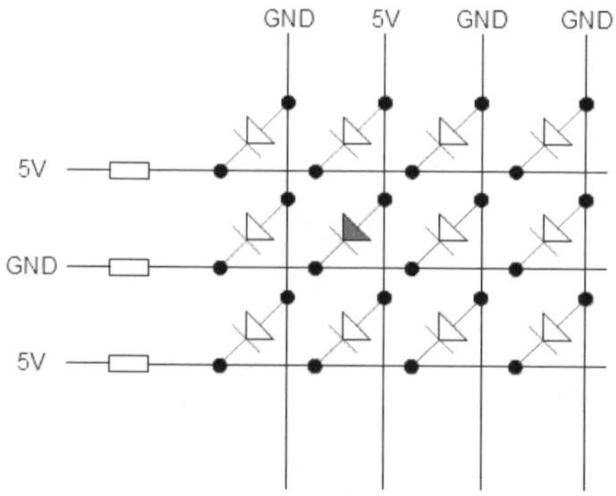

Illustration 42: Operating principle of an LED matrix

The hardware kit includes 10 male to female patch leads. This is not enough to hookup the dot-matrix display which needs 16 connections. You could just use the standard hookup cables with a pin at both ends, holding the pin to the lead on the matrix with some tape or a short length of heat shrink. Unfortunately this quick-fix solution is not too reliable.

It's also possible to solder wires directly to the matrix pins. This will make a more permanent and robust connections especially if the display is mounted inside equipment.

The matrix module pin out (pin 1 is marked on the underside):

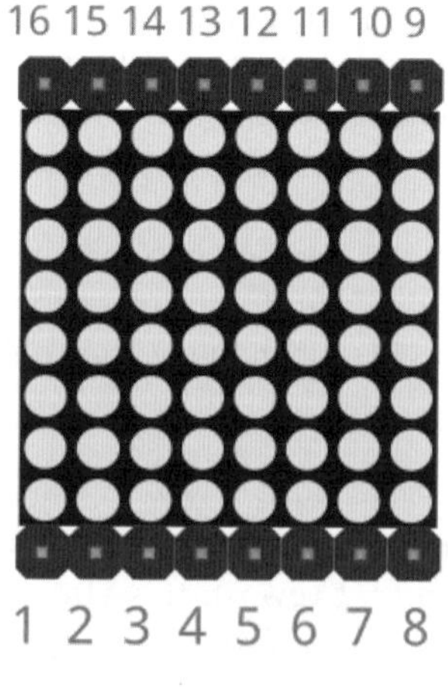

Illustration 43: The dot-matrix module pinout

The table below shows the matrix connections and their connection to the Arduino. The first table shows the pins arranged according to their layout in the matrix. First the row pins (ROW) and then the column pins (COL) are identified.

Row	**1**	**2**	**3**	**4**	**5**	**6**	**7**	**8**
MatrixPin	9	14	8	12	1	7	2	5
Arduino	2	7	19	5	13	18	12	16
Col	**1**	**2**	**3**	**4**	**5**	**6**	**7**	**8**
MatrixPin	13	3	4	10	6	11	15	16
Arduino	6	11	10	3	17	4	8	9

The pins on the matrix module are not obviously arranged in order, to make it more easy for wiring, the following table shows the connections necessary between the Arduino and matrix pins.

Matrix-Pin	1	2	3	4	5	6	7	8
Arduino-Port	13	12	11	10	16	17	18	19

Matrix-Pin	9	10	11	12	13	14	15	16
Arduino-Port	2	3	4	5	6	7	8	9

Finally all the connections including the 220 Ohm series resistors are given in the following illustration.

3.10 The Running Light Spot

The following program lights up one matrix LED after another. It starts at the top left corner and then passes along a column. The same thing happens at the next column and so on. This gives the impression that a point of light runs from left to the right through the display.

If the point of light doesn't behave in this way make a double check of the wiring to the Arduino.

```
// Dot_Matrix_Jumping_dot.ino

// Row   Col 1 2 3 4 5 6 7 8
//  1        o o o o o o o o
//  2        o o o o o o o o
//  3        o o o o o o o o
//  4        o o o o o o o o
//  5        o o o o o o o o
//  6        o o o o o o o o
//  7        o o o o o o o o
//  8        o o o o o o o o

// define row and column pins
int col[8] = {16, 12, 18, 13, 5, 19, 7, 2};     // definition of pin out rows
```

```
int row[8] = {6, 11, 10, 3, 17, 4, 8, 9};        // definition of pin out
columns


void setup()
{ for (int i = 0; i < 8; i++)           // initialize columns 1..8
    {pinMode(col[i], OUTPUT);
     digitalWrite(col[i], LOW);
    }
  for (int i = 0; i < 8; i++)           // initialize row 1..8
    {pinMode(row[i], OUTPUT);
     digitalWrite(row[i], HIGH);
    }
}

void loop()
{ for (int x = 0; x < 8; x++)         // select columns 1..8
    { digitalWrite(col[x], HIGH);
      for (int y = 0; y < 8; y++)     // clear rows 1..8
        digitalWrite(row[y], HIGH);
      for (int y = 0; y < 8; y++)     // set dot @ rows 1..8
      { digitalWrite(row[y], LOW);
        delay(50);
        digitalWrite(row[y], HIGH);
      }
      digitalWrite(col[x], LOW);
    }
}
```

3.11 Beaming Smileys and Glowing Icons

When you're satisfied the dot matrix is connected correctly and the sketch in the last chapter controls the moving spot of light the way it should, we can play a bit more with the displayed symbols. The LED dot-matrix is ideal for displaying icons or basic emojis. Also known as pictograms, they are simple images that, as you know can be used to convey your prevailing mood. Fix the dot-matrix display in a prominent position at the entrance to your room and all visitors will be pre-warned!

All the hardware layout is identical to the previous sketch shown in 3.17. The following sketch will show three different pictograms:

```
// Dot_matrix_ICONS.ino

#include <FrequencyTimer2.h>

#define Heart {{0, 1, 0, 0, 0, 1, 0, 0}, \
               {1, 0, 1, 0, 1, 0, 1, 0}, \
```

```
                {1, 0, 0, 1, 0, 0, 1, 0}, \
                {0, 1, 0, 0, 0, 1, 0, 0}, \
                {0, 0, 1, 0, 1, 0, 0, 0}, \
                {0, 0, 0, 1, 0, 0, 0, 0}, \
                {0, 0, 0, 0, 0, 0, 0, 0}, \
                {0, 0, 0, 0, 0, 0, 0, 0}  \
               }

#define Arrow  {{0, 0, 0, 0, 1, 0, 0, 0}, \
                 {0, 0, 0, 0, 0, 1, 0, 0}, \
                 {0, 0, 0, 0, 0, 0, 1, 0}, \
                 {1, 1, 1, 1, 1, 1, 1, 1}, \
                 {1, 1, 1, 1, 1, 1, 1, 1}, \
                 {0, 0, 0, 0, 0, 0, 1, 0}, \
                 {0, 0, 0, 0, 0, 1, 0, 0}, \
                 {0, 0, 0, 0, 1, 0, 0, 0}  \
                }

#define Anchor {{0, 0, 0, 1, 1, 0, 0, 0}, \
                 {0, 0, 1, 1, 1, 1, 0, 0}, \
                 {0, 0, 0, 1, 1, 0, 0, 0}, \
                 {0, 0, 0, 1, 1, 0, 0, 0}, \
                 {1, 0, 0, 1, 1, 0, 0, 1}, \
                 {1, 0, 0, 1, 1, 0, 0, 1}, \
                 {0, 1, 0, 1, 1, 0, 1, 0}, \
                 {0, 0, 1, 1, 1, 1, 0, 0}  \
                }

#define Space  {{0, 0, 0, 0, 0, 0, 0, 0}, \
                 {0, 0, 0, 0, 0, 0, 0, 0}, \
                 {0, 0, 0, 0, 0, 0, 0, 0}, \
                 {0, 0, 0, 0, 0, 0, 0, 0}, \
                 {0, 0, 0, 0, 0, 0, 0, 0}, \
                 {0, 0, 0, 0, 0, 0, 0, 0}, \
                 {0, 0, 0, 0, 0, 0, 0, 0}, \
                 {0, 0, 0, 0, 0, 0, 0, 0}  \
                }


byte column = 0;
byte LEDs[8][8];

int col[8] = {6, 11, 10, 3, 17, 4, 8, 9};
int row[8] =  {2, 7, 19, 5, 13, 18, 12, 16};

byte patterns[1][8][8] =  { Anchor }; //{ Heart, Arrow, Anchor };
```

```
void setup()
{ for (int i = 2; i <= 19; i++) pinMode(i, OUTPUT);
  for (int i = 1; i <= 8; i++)  digitalWrite(col[i - 1], HIGH);
  for (int i = 1; i <= 8; i++)  digitalWrite(row[i - 1], HIGH);
  clearArray();
  FrequencyTimer2::setPeriod(2000);
  FrequencyTimer2::setOnOverflow(updateDisplay);
  setPattern(0);
}

void loop()
{   setPattern(0);
}

void clearArray()
{ for (int i = 0; i < 8; i++)
  { for (int j = 0; j < 8; j++) LEDs[i][j] = 0;
  }
}

void setPattern(int pattern)
{ for (int i = 0; i < 8; i++)
  { for (int j = 0; j < 8; j++) LEDs[i][j] = patterns[pattern][i][j];
  }
}


void updateDisplay()
{ digitalWrite(col[column], HIGH);
  column++;
  if (column == 8) column = 0;
  for (int r = 0; r < 8; r++)
  { if (LEDs[column][7 - r] == 1) digitalWrite(row[r], HIGH);
    else digitalWrite(row[r], LOW);
  }
  digitalWrite(col[column], LOW);
}
```

Write your choice of icon inside the first set of curly braces

```
byte patterns[1][8][8] =  { Anchor }; //{ Heart, Arrow, Anchor };
```

This is what the heart icon looks like on the display:

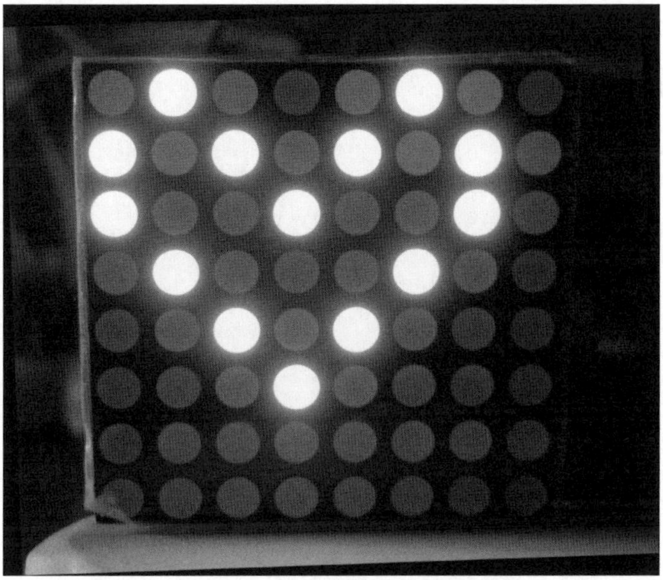

Illustration 44: A dot-matrix heart

The sketch has been organized so you can select one of several icons one after another. The next sketch makes use of the FrequencyTimer2 library; it's an example of how you can show some simple animated graphics.

3.12 Mini Display using an LED Matrix

As we hinted at in the last chapter, as well as a static display the dot-matrix can also used to show a moving image. The Dot_matrix ANIMATION.ino sketch shows a fairly basic animated image on the display. A stylized representation of a face moves its mouth as if it were talking. Used in combination with a voice output from a speaker, it could be a useful add-on for a talking robot project.

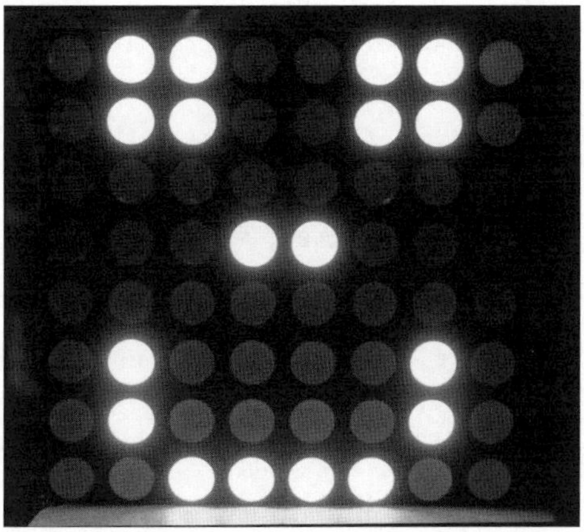

Illustration 45: Smiley

```
// Dot_matrix ANIMATION.ino

#include <FrequencyTimer2.h>

#define B  {{0, 1, 1, 0, 0, 1, 1, 0}, \
            {0, 1, 1, 0, 0, 1, 1, 0}, \
            {0, 0, 0, 0, 0, 0, 0, 0}, \
            {0, 0, 0, 1, 1, 0, 0, 0}, \
            {0, 0, 0, 0, 0, 0, 0, 0}, \
            {0, 0, 0, 0, 0, 0, 0, 0}, \
            {0, 1, 1, 0, 0, 1, 1, 0}, \
            {0, 0, 0, 1, 1, 0, 0, 0}  \
           }

#define H {{0, 1, 1, 0, 0, 1, 1, 0}, \
           {0, 1, 1, 0, 0, 1, 1, 0}, \
           {0, 0, 0, 0, 0, 0, 0, 0}, \
           {0, 0, 0, 1, 1, 0, 0, 0}, \
           {0, 0, 0, 0, 0, 0, 0, 0}, \
           {0, 0, 0, 0, 0, 0, 0, 0}, \
           {0, 0, 1, 1, 1, 1, 0, 0}, \
           {0, 0, 0, 1, 1, 0, 0, 0}  \
          }

#define O {{0, 1, 1, 0, 0, 1, 1, 0}, \
           {0, 1, 1, 0, 0, 1, 1, 0}, \
           {0, 0, 0, 0, 0, 0, 0, 0}, \
           {0, 0, 0, 1, 1, 0, 0, 0}, \
           {0, 0, 0, 0, 0, 0, 0, 0}, \
           {0, 0, 0, 1, 1, 0, 0, 0}, \
           {0, 0, 1, 0, 0, 1, 0, 0}, \
           {0, 0, 0, 1, 1, 0, 0, 0}  \
          }

#define S {{0, 1, 1, 0, 0, 1, 1, 0}, \
           {0, 1, 1, 0, 0, 1, 1, 0}, \
           {0, 0, 0, 0, 0, 0, 0, 0}, \
           {0, 0, 0, 1, 1, 0, 0, 0}, \
           {0, 0, 0, 0, 0, 0, 0, 0}, \
           {0, 1, 0, 0, 0, 0, 1, 0}, \
           {0, 1, 0, 0, 0, 0, 1, 0}, \
           {0, 0, 1, 1, 1, 1, 0, 0}  \
          }

byte column = 0;
byte LEDs[8][8];
```

```
int col[8] = {6, 11, 10, 3, 17, 4, 8, 9};
int row[8] =  {2, 7, 19, 5, 13, 18, 12, 16};

const int numPatterns = 4;
byte patterns[numPatterns][8][8] = { S, H, B, O };
int pattern = 0;

void setup()
{ for (int i = 2; i <= 19; i++) pinMode(i, OUTPUT);
  for (int i = 1; i <= 8; i++)  digitalWrite(col[i - 1], HIGH);
  for (int i = 1; i <= 8; i++)  digitalWrite(row[i - 1], HIGH);
  clearArray();
  FrequencyTimer2::setPeriod(2000);
  FrequencyTimer2::setOnOverflow(updateDisplay);
  setPattern(pattern);
}

void loop()
{   pattern = ++pattern % numPatterns;
    setPattern(pattern);
    delay(200);
    clearArray();
}

void clearArray()
{ for (int i = 0; i < 8; i++)
  { for (int j = 0; j < 8; j++) LEDs[i][j] = 0;
  }
}

void setPattern(int pattern)
{ for (int i = 0; i < 8; i++)
  { for (int j = 0; j < 8; j++) LEDs[i][j] = patterns[pattern][i][j];
  }
}

void updateDisplay()
{ digitalWrite(col[column], HIGH);
  column++;
  if (column == 8) column = 0;
  for (int r = 0; r < 8; r++)
  { if (LEDs[column][7 - r] == 1) digitalWrite(row[r], HIGH);
    else digitalWrite(row[r], LOW);
  }
  digitalWrite(col[column], LOW);
}
```

3.13 A Joystick-controlled light point

This project requires a component we haven't used before. The joystick module contains two potentiometers moved by a central stick. A switch function is also incorporated and is activated by pressing down on the stick.

The module has five connections. The following table summarizes their function and shows how to connect them to the Arduino.

Module pin	**Arduino pin**	**Function**
P5V	P5V	Supply voltage
GND	GND	Ground
VRx	z. B. A0	x-Potentiometer output
VRy	z. B. A1	y-Potentiometer output
SW	Any Digital pin	Switch function

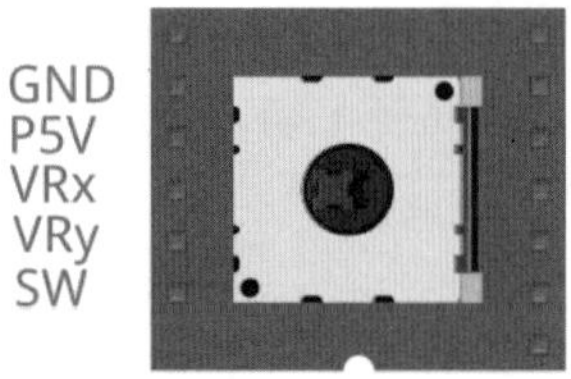

Illustration 46: The Joystick

The joystick is a commonly used component in the world of model making to provide the control input for hand-held transmitters to steer model cars, aircraft, drones and ships.

In this project, the joystick controls the movement of a light spot on the LED dot-matrix. The joystick therefore gives two-dimensional control of the light spot. It also illustrates the functional principle by which many video games work.

Illustration 47: The Joystick module

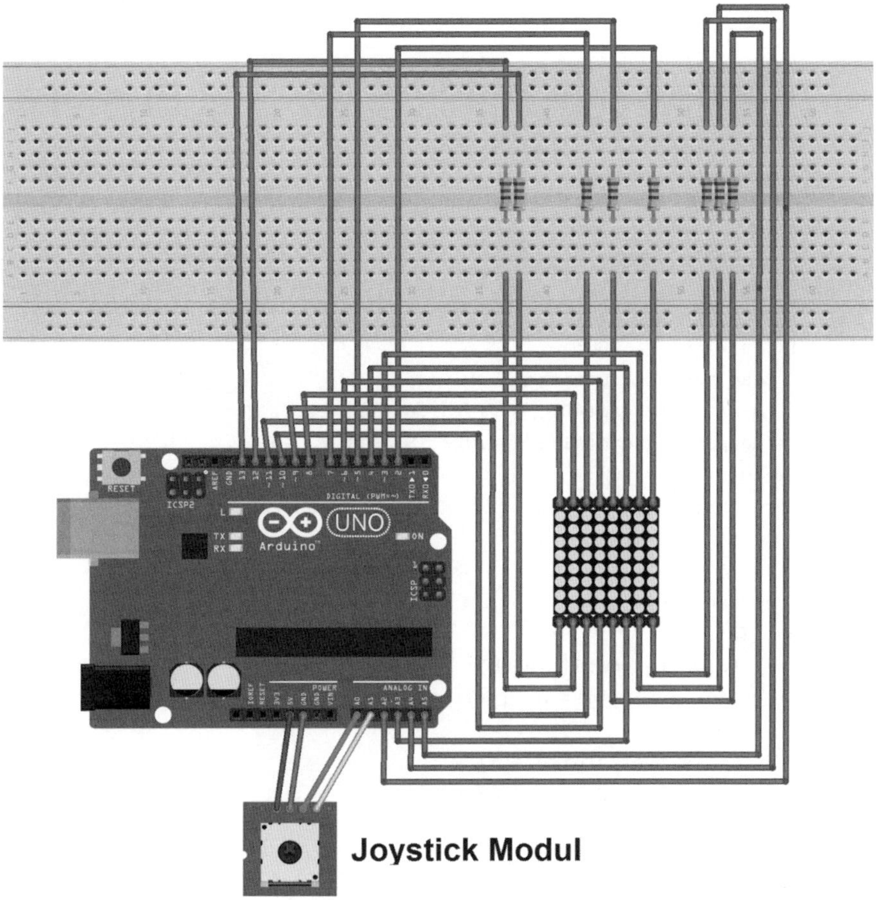

Illustration 48: The joystick controls the light spot

The sketch to control the light spot on the dot matrix display looks like this:

```
// Dot matrix control.ino
// Dot matric control via joystick

const int row[8] = { 2, 7, 19, 5, 13, 18, 12, 16 };
const int col[8] = { 6, 11, 10, 3, 17, 4, 8, 9 };

int pixels[8][8];
int x = 5, y = 5;

void setup()
{  for (int i = 0; i < 8; i++)
  {  pinMode(col[i], OUTPUT);
     pinMode(row[i], OUTPUT);
     digitalWrite(col[i], HIGH);
```

```
    }
    // initialize matrix
    for (int x = 0; x < 8; x++)
    { for (int y = 0; y < 8; y++)
      {  pixels[x][y] = HIGH; }
    }
}

void loop()
{   // turn off the last position:
    pixels[x][y] = HIGH;
    // read joystick position
    x = map(analogRead(A0), 0, 1023, 0, 7);
    y = map(analogRead(A1), 0, 1023, 0, 7);
    pixels[x][y] = LOW;
    refreshMatrix();
}

void refreshMatrix() {
    for (int i = 0; i < 8; i++)
    { digitalWrite(row[i], HIGH);
      for (int j = 0; j < 8; j++)
      { // pixel on
       int thisPixel = pixels[i][j];
        digitalWrite(col[j], thisPixel);
        // pixel off
        if (thisPixel == LOW) {
          digitalWrite(col[j], HIGH);
        }
      }
      // clear row:
      digitalWrite(row[i], LOW);
    }
}
```

Chapter 4 • Measuring the Environment

Monitoring and taking measurements of our environment are some of the most important technological tasks of the modern age. Whether it's tied up with vehicle emissions, protection of the environmental or in the field of robotics. It's becoming increasingly important to have accurate information on the conditions of both our local and remote environments.

4.1 Dry Out the Cellar: Hygrometer Monitors Humidity.

The hardware kit includes a combined temperature and humidity sensor. Along with the two sensors this component also includes the necessary A/D converter to provide both measurements as digital values. This makes it really easy to use. Communication with the sensor including the transfer of all measured values takes place over a single data pin. The sensor unit itself has four pins, one of which is not connected so altogether we use just three connections, two of which are to supply power. The data signal also has a pull up resistor on board.

The two illustrations below show the module and its corresponding pin outs.

Illustration 49: DHT11Temperature/Humidity sensor

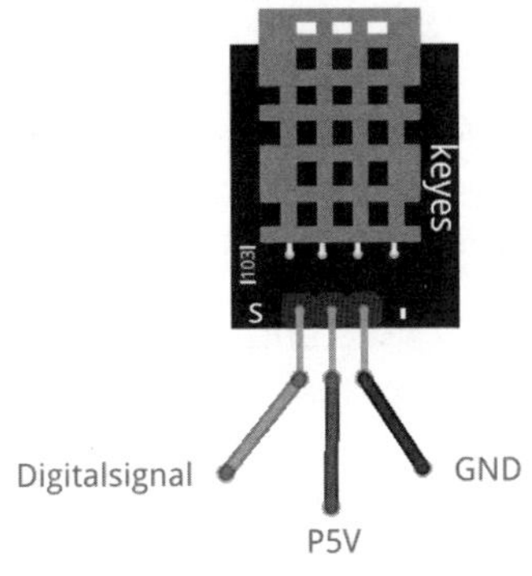

Illustration 50: The DHT11 measures Temperature and Humidity

The following table shows the sensors operating temperature and humidity ranges:

Temperature range	0 - 50 °C
Temperature accuracy	±2 °C
Humidity range	20 - 90 % % Rel. Humidity
Humidity accuracy	±5 % % Rel. Humidity

A suitable library for use with this sensor can be downloaded for free from:

http://arduino.cc/playground/Main/DHTLib

The read() function in this library returns the following values:

- DHTLIB_OK (0): Sensor value and check sum OK.
- DHTLIB_ERROR_CHECKSUM (-1): Check sum error
- DHTLIB_ERROR_TIMEOUT (-2): Time out

Using the library makes it easy to read sensor information:

```
// DHT11_test.ino

#include <dht.h>
dht DHT;
#define DHT11_PIN 4

void setup()
{ Serial.begin(9600);
  // Serial.println("Type,\tstatus,\tHumidity (%),\tTemperature (C)");
}

void loop()
{ DHT.read11(DHT11_PIN);
  Serial.print("Humidity: "); Serial.print(DHT.humidity,0); Serial.
println(" %");
  Serial.print("Temperature: "); Serial.print(DHT.temperature,0); Serial.
println(" C");
  Serial.println();
  delay(1000);
}
```

As you can see the circuit is really simple to hook up. The sensor just connects to the Arduino via three lines. You can choose a different Arduino input pin to transfer the data. To do this you will also need to change the pin definition in the sketch to the new pin number so that it can communicate successfully with the module:

```
#define DHT11_PIN 4
```

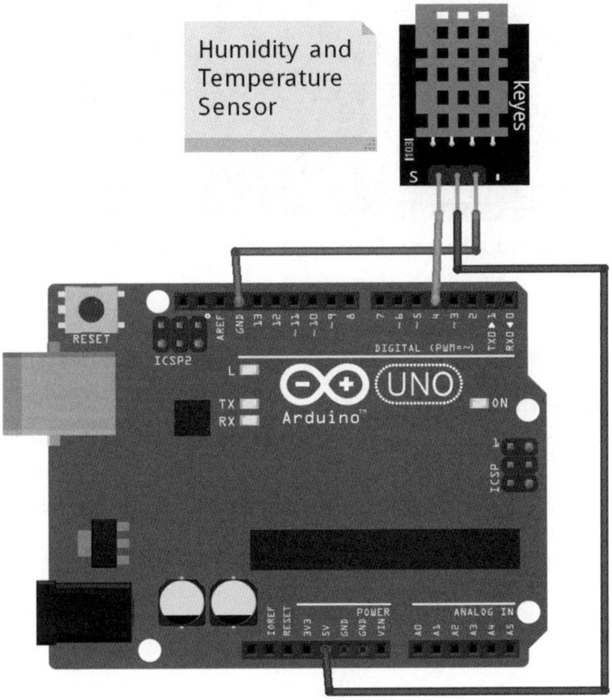

Illustration 51: The Hygrometer provides precise humidity measurements

The measured values can be viewed using the Serial Monitor in the Arduino IDE. To display the values on another PC it will be necessary to run a terminal emulator program like Tera-Term on the PC. A terminal emulator program used to be part of the standard Windows environment but with more recent versions of Windows it needs to be installed. Tera-Term can be downloaded from:

http://ttssh2.osdn.jp/index.html.en

The output data in Tera Term looks like this:

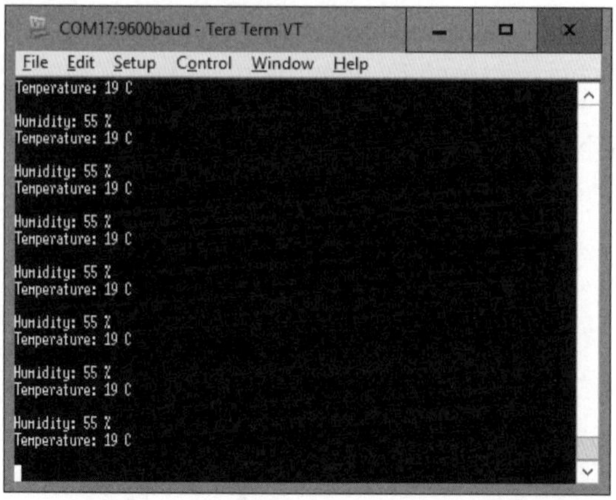

Illustration 52: Data output displayed using a serial terminal program.

It is necessary to set the correct COM port number and baud rate for communication with the Arduino.

4.2 Weather Station with LC Display

In many cases, of course, you don't always want to fire up a complete PC or laptop just because you want to know the room temperature or the current humidity. This is where the LC-Display is useful. Thanks to its serial interface, it can be used in parallel with the DHT11 to make a stand-alone weather station.
The program looks like this:

```
// DHT11_w_LCD_display.ino

#include <dht.h>
#include <LiquidCrystal_I2C.h>
#include <Wire.h>
LiquidCrystal_I2C lcd(0x27,16,2);  // set the LCD address to 0x27 for a 16
chars and 2 line display
dht DHT;
const int DHT11_PIN= 4;
void setup()
{ lcd.begin();  //initialize the lcd
  lcd.backlight();  //open the backlight
}

void loop()
{ DHT.read11(DHT11_PIN);

  lcd.setCursor(0, 0); lcd.print("Temp:      "); lcd.print(DHT.
temperature,0);
  lcd.print(char(223));//print the unit" ⊠ "
  lcd.print("C");
```

```
    lcd.setCursor(0, 1);
    lcd.print("Humidity:  ");
    lcd.print(DHT.humidity,0); lcd.print(" %");
    delay(200);
  }
```

All the required libraries were installed earlier.

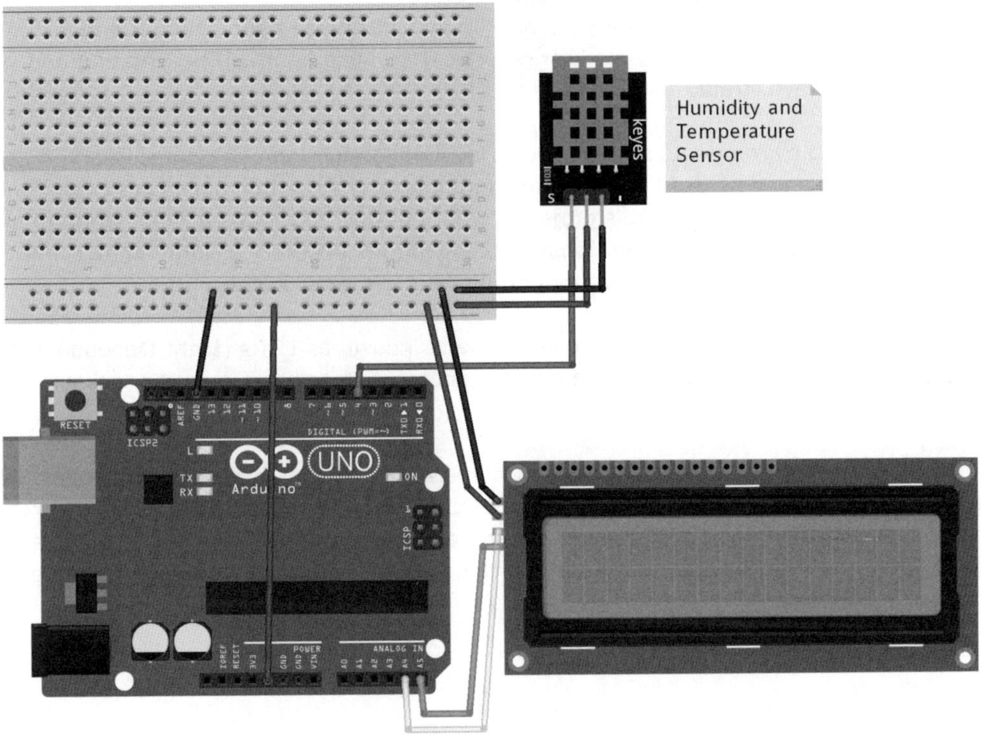

Illustration 53: Weather station with LC Display

The hardware can also be quickly wired up. All the units can be mounted in a suitable case to make a useful tabletop unit. Additional sensors could also be added to the system allowing other environmental variables such as outside air temperature and air pressure to be measured and displayed.

Illustration 54: Displayed sensor data

4.3 Workplace Bright Enough? A Digital Lux Meter.

As well as temperature and humidity it's also important to make sure there is enough light to make a space comfortable to work or relax in. Too much light can be irritating and too little can lead to eye strain.

In many working evironments a very specific level of lighting intensity is necessary. A calibrated light meter can be used to record the light intensity at certain points in a room. With an experimental setup such as this project it's not possible to measure illumination to any legally prescribed precision. We don't have access to the necessary calibration tools but we won't let that stop us from building a brightness meter that is still very useful.

Included in the hardware kit are three components known as LDRs (**L**ight **D**ependant **R**esistors) or photoresistors. The resistance of a photoresistor changes as the incident light level changes.

As the light level increases the LDR's electrical resistance drops. This is due to the so-called photoelectric effect exhibited by the materials used to build the LDR. LDRs tend to react relatively slowly to changing light levels but some of the more recently introduced versions are much better in this respect. The LDRs included with the kit are however well suited to measuring light levels.

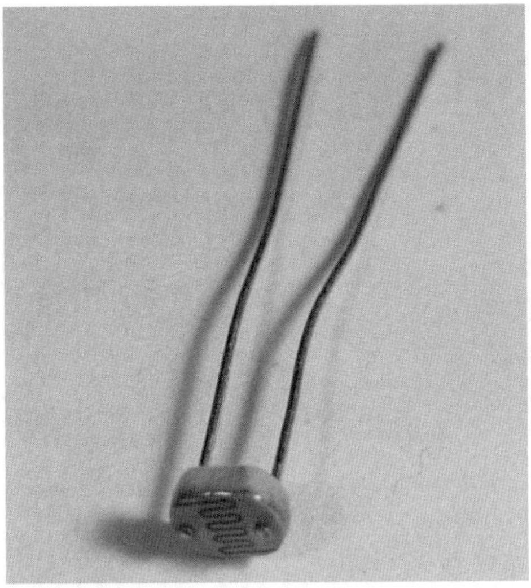

Illustration 55: Photoresistor (LDR)

The LDR is used together with a fixed resistor forming a basic voltage divider configuration to produce an analog voltage level measured by the Arduino. This illustration shows the simple circuit hookup with the Arduino.

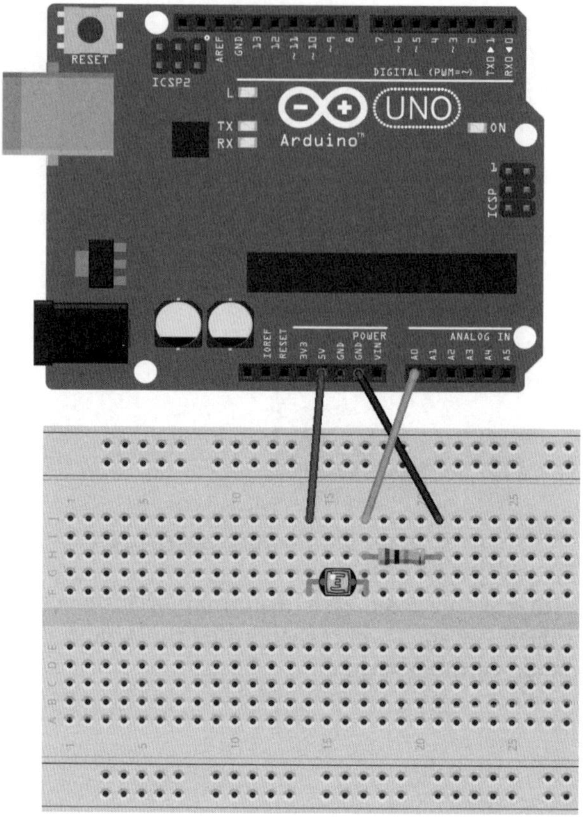

Illustration 56: The Arduino light meter

The sketch reads the digital values of the internal A/D converter in the controller at the heart of the Arduino board. The value is only normalized to 100%. The Arduino's ADC uses 10 bits which gives output values in the range from 0 to $2^{10}-1$ = 1023. The calibration factor is therefore 1023 / 100 = 10.23.

```
// LDR_Luxmeter.ino

int intensity;
int ADC_0=0;

void setup()
{ Serial.begin(9600);
}

void loop()
{ intensity=analogRead(ADC_0);
  Serial.print("Brightness: ");
  Serial.print(intensity/10.23);
```

```
    Serial.println(" %");
    delay(1000);
  }
```

Click on the Serial Monitor to see the brightness readings. Under normal lighting level conditions we can expect a measured value in the range from 20 to 70 %. Moving the LDR closer to a table lamp you can expect the readings to approach 100 %. In complete darkness the value drops close to 0 %.

The instrument can also be a useful tool for hobby photographers. Even with all the bells and whistles availble on modern digital cameras it's important that the subject is optimally lit to get the best results. With a little practice and experimentation the homebrew light meter can help improve the quality of your photo images.

Chapter 5 • Sensor Technology

Sensors or probes are components that are sensitive to certain physical or chemical properties. Important examples of electronically measurable variables are:

- Temperature
- Humidity
- Light intensity
- Pressure
- Sound intensity
- Thermal radiation
- Power or Acceleration
- Magnetism or magnetic field

Sensors are used in every branch of technology. A typical motor car will contain over 100 different sensors. In fact there is hardly any area of high tech that doesn't make use of them. From space travel to medical technology, from smart phones to industrial automation they all rely on information gathered by these sophisticated transducers.
In the previous chapter we've already used sensors to measure light intensity and air temperature. In the following sections we expand the area of application by using some new sensors for

- Flame detection
- Tilt sensing
- Noise level detection

Usually a single sensor is used to make a specific measurement. The value produced must be reproducible and is usually expressed as a voltage level or a change in resistance of the sensor. In general it's preferable for the sensor to produce an output value which has a linear relationship to the measured variable. Some sensors however may have a non-linear characteristic but it's easy to convert the values in the microcontroller software.
Some external activity can introduce inaccuracies in sensor readings. This is an effect known as cross-sensitivity where a sensor's measurements are affected by other unrelated variables. Some examples are:

- Influence of air humidity on electric field strength measurements
- Temperature influences on light sensors
- The influence of mechanical vibrations on sound transducers
- Thermal effects on humidity or pressure sensors

A lot of effort can go into minimizing the influence these unwanted variables can have on the measured values. A common technique is to measure the interfering variable directly and use this value to provide a mathematical correction to the wanted variable. The humidity module we used earlier contains inbuilt temperature compensation so there is no need for the user to make any further correction to its measured values.

It's good practice however to always check to what extent cross-sensitivity can influence the required measurement precision of any sensor you plan to use.

5.1 The Flame Detector

The flame detector is a special type of opto-sensor similar to one we used in a previous project. It is sensitive to sources of infrared light (from around 750 to 1100 nm) and reacts particularly strongly to naked flames. Most of the visible light is filtered by the special dark plastic package surrounding the light-sensing area. This makes the detector look like a black LED and should make it easy to identify. Despite the strong filter the detector can still be influenced by visible light, special measures must therefore be taken in order to ensure it can reliably detect a flame.

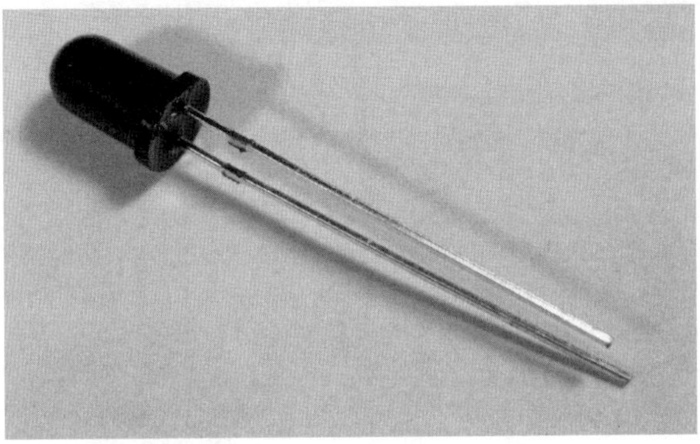

Illustration 57: The flame sensor

Flame sensors are widely used in equipment such as gas boilers where they play an important safety role to quickly shut off gas to the boiler if they detect the flame has gone out. Without this safety mechanism the room would fill with gas and present a serious risk of explosion.

In principle the flame sensor is nothing more than an IR photo diode sensitive to the infra red radiation produced by a naked flame. The sensor has a sensitive acceptance cone of approximately 60° around its central axis.

In the circuit the IR diode is reverse-bias connected with a series 10 Kohm resistor. This configuration makes a voltage divider network producing a voltage level which we read at one of the Arduino's analog inputs. The illustration shows how the flame sensor is connected to the Arduino.

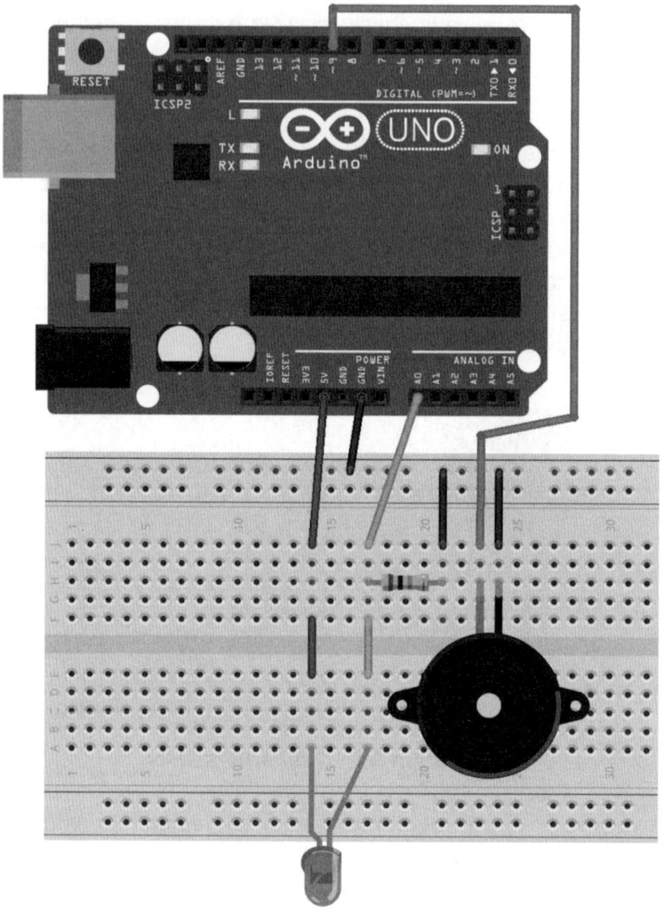

Illustration 58: Flame Alarm

In addition to the sensor itself, the piezoelectric sound transducer is also used here. This creates a system to sound an alarm when a flame is detected. You could set up the sensor so that it only detects the flame when a candle has burnt down to a certain point and thereby triggers the alarm. Be aware that unattended candles are a fire hazard; make sure that the flame cannot come into contact with any other combustible material.

WARNING: All of the circuits described here must only be used for the purposes of experimentation and learning. The publisher and author cannot be held responsible for their inappropriate use. The flame detector is not suitable for use as a fire detector alarm and is not a safety device!

In the corresponding sketch the Arduino analog input pin A0 is used to measure the voltage produced at the IR sensor. A level of brightness represented by the integer value 'threshold' is used to determine at what point the alarm will trigger. The Arduino built-in LED13 is also turned on at the same time the alarm sounds.

The input signal level from the sensor is also sent to the serial monitor interface so you can easily see the values and set a different threshold level as necessary.

Illustration 59: Monitoring a candle flame

```
// Flame_alarm.ino
// Rv = 10 k

#define AlarmLED 13
#define speaker 9

int ADC_value;
int ADC_0=0;
int threshold = 300;

void setup()
{ Serial.begin(9600);
  pinMode(AlarmLED, OUTPUT);
}

void loop()
{ ADC_value=analogRead(ADC_0);
  Serial.println(ADC_value);

  if(ADC_value > threshold)
    { digitalWrite(AlarmLED,HIGH);
      tone(speaker,1000,100);
      Serial.println("Flame alert!");
    }
  else digitalWrite(AlarmLED,LOW);
  delay(300);
}
```

The sensor is also sensitive to the light emitted by filament lamps which as well as visible light also emit energy in the infra red region of the spectrum. Other light sources such as energy-saving lamps and LEDs emit much less IR energy and will not interfere so much with the flame measurement. This clearly shows the improved efficiency of more modern lighting technology which emits less energy in the IR region of the spectrum.

5.2 Alarm system with tilt switch

The tilt switch is one of the most basic types of sensor available. It can be attached to an object and be used to indicate when the object is moved. The illustration shows how the sensor works.

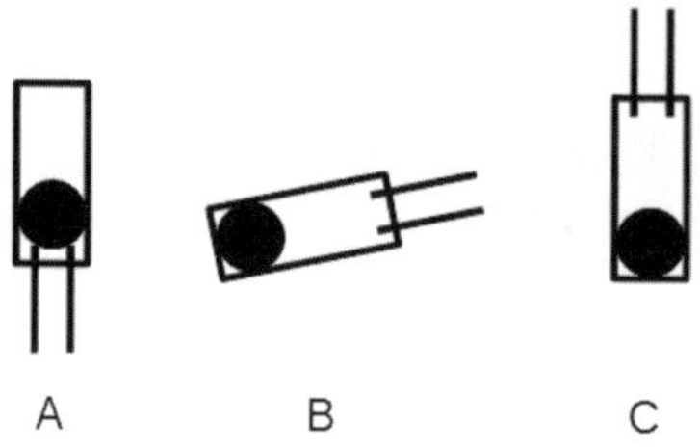

Illustration 60: How the tilt switch works

Its operating principle is very simple: a conductive ball can roll backwards and forwards inside a tube, at one end of the tube are two electrodes, when the ball rolls to this end it completes the circuit between them:

a: contact closed
b. contact breaks
c: contact open

The state of the tilt switch contacts can be determined using a digital I/O pin on the Arduino. The following illustration shows how the tilt switch can be hooked up to an Arduino to make an alarm unit.

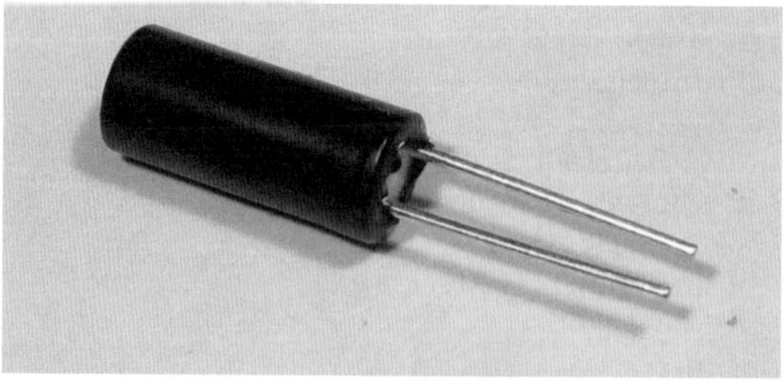

Illustration 61: The tilt switch

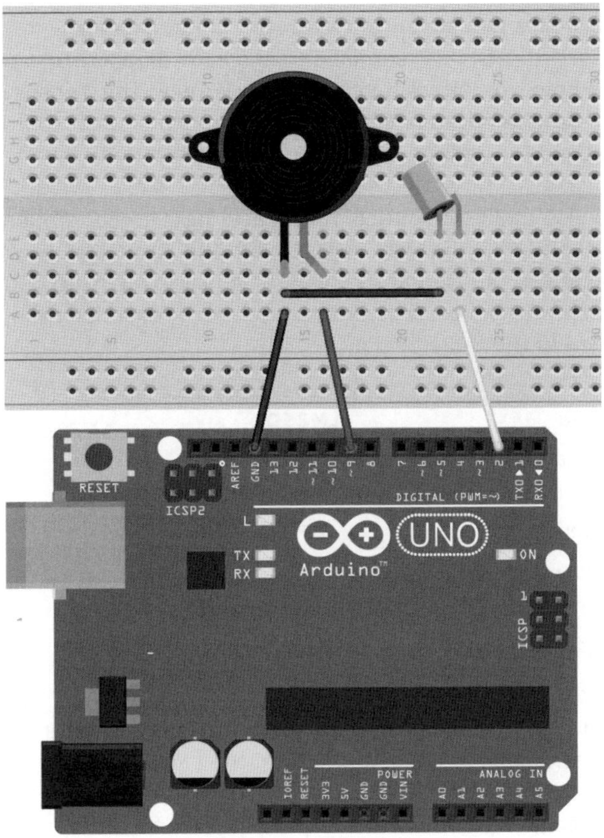

Illustration 62: Tilt alarm

The sketch just tests the voltage level at the input pin. When it's LOW the alarm signal is sounded:

```
// Tilt_alarm.ino

int speaker = 9;

void setup()
{ pinMode(speaker, OUTPUT);
  pinMode(2, INPUT_PULLUP);
}

void loop()
{ if(digitalRead(2) == LOW)
    { tone(speaker,1000,100);
    }
  delay(300);
}
```

5.3 Precise Temperature Measurement with the LM35 Sensor

We have already used the DHT11 combined sensor to measure temperature. The LM35 temperature sensor however, offers much better accuracy. This sensor is completely packaged in a transistor-outline package which makes it much smaller than the DHT11 sensor. This allows it to be used in confined, difficult-to-access locations.

The package shape also makes it suitable for measuring surface temperatures. For this application the sensor should be in direct contact with the surface to be measured. A special heat-conducting paste can be used at the point of contact to ensure optimum heat transfer to improve the measurement accuracy and temperature response time. The main features of the LM35 are given in the table below:

Type	**LM35DZ**
Package outline	TO-92, (like small-signal transistor)
Temperature range	-55°C to +150°C
Supply voltage	4 to 5.5V (max. 30V)
Accuracy	0.5°C at 25°C
Calibration factor	10mV/°C

A simple NTC thermistor could also be used to measure temperature but the LM35 offers some significant advantages. The main one is that the LM35 leaves the factory already precisely calibrated; in contrast each NTC thermistor has slightly different characteristics and must be individually calibrated before it can produce any accurate readings. An integrated sensor such as the LM35 eliminates this requirement completely. It supplies a precise output voltage with a linear characteristic of 10 mV/°C.

To improve the measurement accuracy you can thermally decouple the leads to the sensor so that readings will not be affected by heat reaching the sensor via its leads.

Connecting the LM35 to the Arduino is also really easy. It just requires +5V, ground and an analog input pin.

The following illustrations include a photo of the components, the wiring layout and construction of a complete electronic thermometer with an LC display.

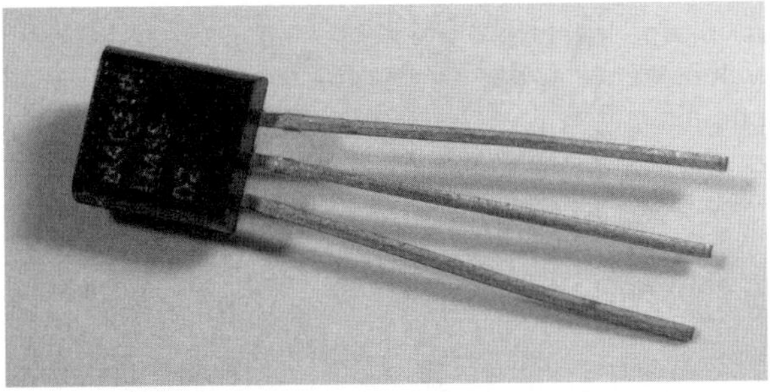

Illustration 63: The LM35 temperature sensor

The following Illustration shows the pin outs in detail.

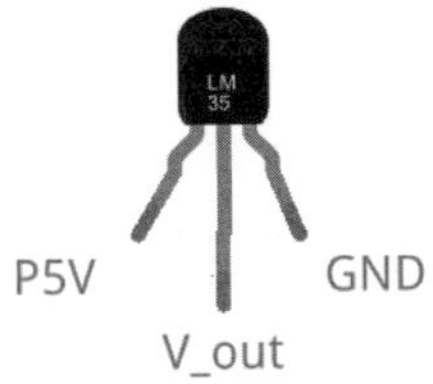

Illustration 64: Pin assignments of the LM35

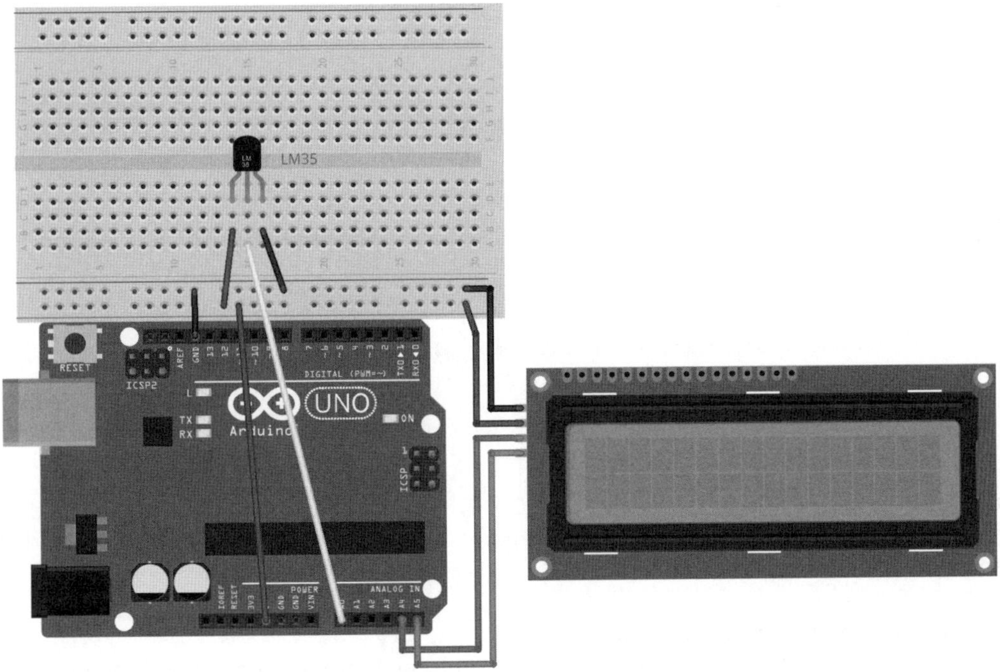

Illustration 65: A complete electronic thermometer using the LM35

To display the output voltage level from the sensor as a temperature in °C it will be necessary to convert the value. As we already know the Uno has a 10-bit ADC which means the maximum value will be exactly

$$2^{10}-1 = 1023$$

which corresponds to an output voltage of 5 V. The conversion factor is therefore given as

```
(5 / 1023) / 10 mV/°C = 0.00489 / 0.01 V/°C = 0.489 V/°C
```

The complete program looks like this:

```
// LM35_w_LCD.ino

#include <Wire.h>
#include <LiquidCrystal_I2C.h>
LiquidCrystal_I2C lcd(0x27,16,2);  // set the LCD address to 0x27 for a 16
chars and 2 line display

float temp = 0;
long LM35val = 0;

void setup()
{
  lcd.begin();  //initialize the lcd
  lcd.backlight();  //open the backlight
}
void loop()
{ LM35val = analogRead(A0);
  temp = (LM35val * 0.489);
  lcd.setCursor(0,0); lcd.print("LM35 Temperature");
  lcd.setCursor(1,1); lcd.print("Temp = ");
  lcd.setCursor(7,1); lcd.print(temp, 1);   // one decimal
  lcd.print(" "); lcd.print(char(223)); lcd.print("C");
  delay(200);
}
```

The temperature reading is shown on the LCD. The complete unit can be mounted inside a suitable case to make a precise digital thermometer which should prove useful around the home or in the lab.

5.4 Measuring low Temperatures

To test the sensor at measuring very low temperatures there are a number of options you can try:

- Cooling by alcohol evaporation
- Cool packs

The first option achieves cooling without the use of a fridge. Just wrap the sensor in a small strip of material or cotton wool and let a few drops of pure alcohol soak into it. Blowing on the material or the use of a fan will produce evaporative cooling and you will see a corresponding drop in the displayed temperature reading.

A small cold bath can be made up from a mixture of crushed ice and table salt. Better still use de-icing salt, you should be able to achieve an ice bath temperature of below -18 °C using this method.

Even simpler would be to use a coolbox ice pack stored in a freezer or even a squirt of Servisol freezer spray (normally used in the lab for fault-finding) to achieve temperatures down to -50 °C.

An example application measuring low temperatures:

Illustration 66: Sensing in the deep freeze

5.5 Shout or whisper - measure the level with a sound sensor

Another very interesting module in the kit is the sound sensor. This has a sensitive electret microphone together with a matching amplifier.

Illustration 67: The sound sensor-module

This sensor is highly sensitive and can pickup all sorts of noises. The module has two outputs:

AO: An analog output signal i.e. the amplified microphone signal.

DO: Digital output: When the sound intensity exceeds a preset threshold level this output switches from a LOW to a HIGH level.

The sensitivity of the module can be adjusted with a potentiometer. The following waveforms show the two output signals. The upper trace is the analog output signal at A0 and the lower trace the digital output signal DO. It can be seen that the digital signal switches to a HIGH whenever the analog signal exceeds a certain threshold.

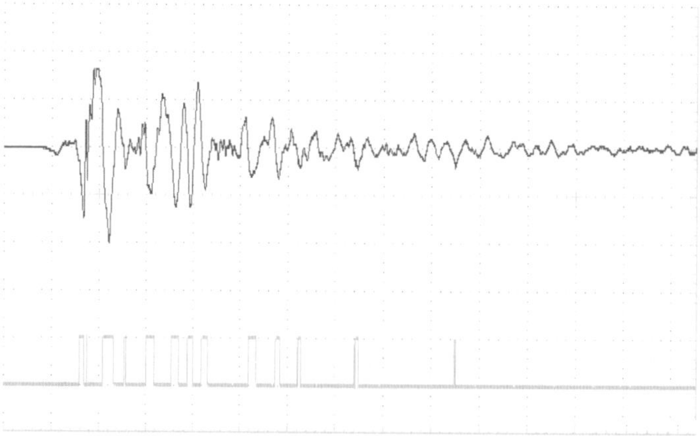

Illustration 68: Output waveforms from the microphone module

Connections between the module and Arduino can be made using the male-female hookup cables included in the kit. The table below gives the connections:

Sound sensor module	**Arduino**
DO: Digital Output	D 08 etc.
DA: Analog Output	A0 etc.
'+' : P5V	5V
'G' : GND	GND

The setup can be seen in the photo below.

In the simplest case the analog signal can be connected to the Serial Plotter available under the tools tab in the IDE. The baudrate is increased to 115200 to provide higher data transfer rate, make sure you set the plotter to the same rate by clicking on the tab in the lower left corner.

```
The sketch is given here:

// Sound_sensor_analog.ino

const int analogInPin = A0;

int sensorValue = 0;

void setup()
{   Serial.begin(115200);
}

void loop()
{ sensorValue = analogRead(analogInPin);
  Serial.println(sensorValue);
}
```

After the sketch has been loaded to the Arduino the Serial Plotter can be started. The plotter function was added to the Arduino IDE from build version 1.6.6 and is a low bandwidth oscilloscope feature, useful for showing low frequency signals. The plotter display now shows waveforms of all the sounds that the microphone picks up.

The serial plotter is a very basic type of oscilloscope with quite a low bandwidth. Low frequency sounds are represented quite well but higher frequencies cannot be displayed with the same accuracy and don't really look anything like the actual signal coming from the microphone module. To get a better view you will need to use a real oscilloscope with a bandwidth of at least 1 MHz.

Illustration 69: The sound waveform shown using the Serial Plotter

5.6 Remote Control without a Transmitter: The intelligent Clap Switch

Clap switches were one of the first novelty applications to be built by hobby electronics enthusiasts. They are useful in many applications and were usually designed using analog components. One popular application was to use it as a 'party-effect' switch which turns off all the lights for a few seconds when it detects a hand clap... I can't imagine why this was useful.

The simple analog clap switch, however, had a big disadvantage in that they reacted to every sudden sound. As a real "remote control" unit they really had quite limited usefulness.

Using a microcontroller gives you many more possibilities. You could arrange it so that you need to clap your hands 3 times in rapid succession to activate a relay for example. A loud sound can, of course occur naturally such as when a door slams but the chances of three such events occuring in rapid succession is less likely. The Arduino can be used to count the pulses and therfore significantly improves operational reliability.

The following illustration shows how the parts are hooked up to register and count the sounds:

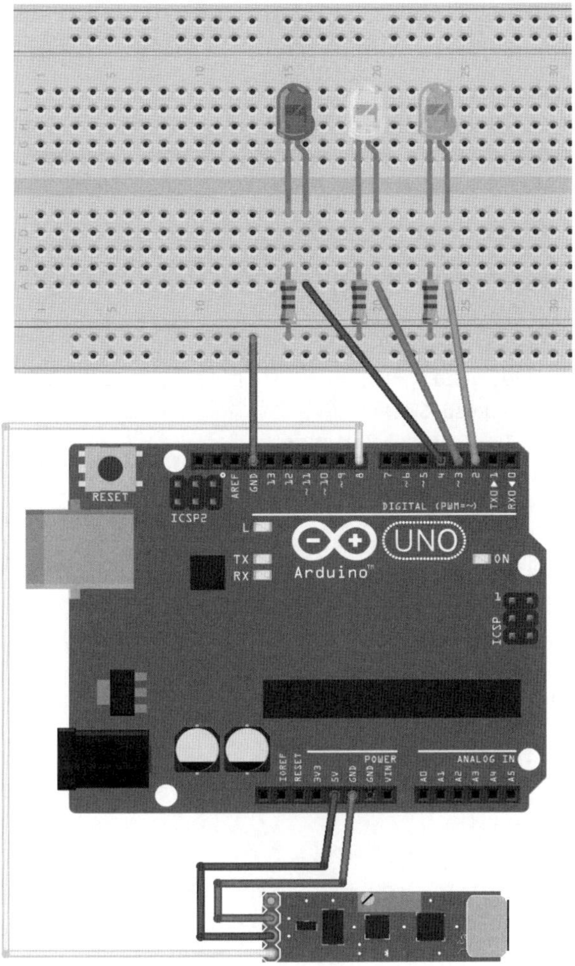

Illustration 70:The clap switch

This sketch is a little more complex:

```
// Clapping_Switch.ino

#define LED1 2   // 1x clap - 1. LED
#define LED2 3   // 2x clap - 2. LED
#define LED3 4   // 3x clap - 3. LED or relay etc
#define SW1 8    // Input for clap signal

#define T1  10  // delay
#define T2  100  // ON-Time of 3. LED
#define T3  10   // reset-delay
#define C1  300  // loop constant
```

```
void setup()
{  pinMode(SW1,INPUT);
   digitalWrite(SW1,HIGH);   // activate internal pull-up
   pinMode(LED1,OUTPUT); pinMode(LED2,OUTPUT); pinMode(LED3,OUTPUT);
}

void loop()
{ if(digitalRead(SW1))
  {  digitalWrite(LED1, HIGH);
     delay(T1);
     for(int n=0; n<C1; n++)
     { if(digitalRead(SW1))
       { digitalWrite(LED2, HIGH);
         delay(T1);
         for(int m=0; m<C1; m++)
         { if(digitalRead(SW1))
           { digitalWrite(LED3, HIGH);
             for(int q=0; q<10; q++)
             delay(T2);
           }
           delay(T3);
         }
         delay(T3);
       }
       delay(T3);
     }
     digitalWrite(LED1, LOW);
     digitalWrite(LED2, LOW);
     digitalWrite(LED3, LOW);
  }
}
```

5.7 Rain or shine? A water level sensor can alert you

A water level or drip sensor can be used for a number of applications. The sensing element is able to detect the presence of any liquid which is conductive. It only needs a few drops of liquid on the sensing element to detect it.

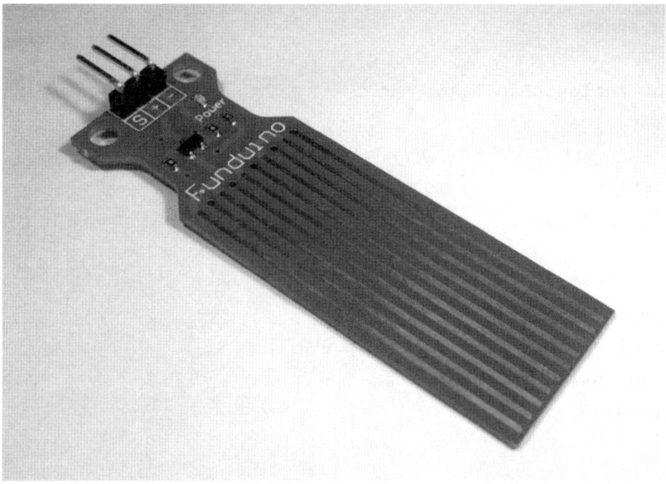

Illustration 71: The water level sensor

One important application of this sensor is as a rain sensor. As soon as the first few drops rain fall on the sensor it can trigger the Arduino to automatically close a roof window or operate an awning mechanism. It can also generate an acoustic or visual alarm warning you to bring the washing in before it gets soaked. This kind of signal is also used for vehicle technology, on most modern cars the windshield wipers are automatically controlled via a rain sensor. The driver isn't distracted and can concentrate on driving.

The functional principle of the rain sensor is based on a conductivity measurement. As soon as a liquid completes a circuit between two silver contact strips which make up the sensing element, a small amount of current flows. This is amplified by a transistor to produce a changing voltage level. The sensor outputs an analog signal at pin 'S' of the module.

When the sensor surface is completely dry, the output is at 0 V. A single drop of water on the sensor element produces an output of half the supply voltage. The more liquid on the sensor, the higher the voltage value becomes. If the element is completely immersed in water, almost the full operating voltage will appear at the sensor output.

This table shows the connections between the Arduino and sensor:

Sensor pin	**Arduino pin**
+	5 V
-	GND
S	A0

In this first sketch, the sensor values are digitized in the Arduino and output to the serial monitor or plotter.

```
// Fluid_sensor.ino

const int analogInPin = A0;
int sensorValue = 0;

void setup()
{ Serial.begin(9600);
}

void loop()
{ sensorValue = analogRead(analogInPin);
  Serial.println(sensorValue);
  delay(100);
}
```

In this next project, an alarm is triggered as soon as a drop is detected on the sensor.

5.8 Umbrella alert! – A rainfall alarm

This bit of kit should prove indispensible in the hallway to let you know whether it's wet or fine outside. When it starts raining the alarm activates and gives you a warning you will need to take your brolly or waterproof with you. In this sketch the alarm threshold level is set to 300 but you can experiment by changing this to a different value as necessary.

In addition to the water level sensor this project also uses a piezo buzzer connected at pin 9. This is used to produce an alarm sound when a water level is detected (see illustration 5.6 also). An LED is also used to give a visual alert.

You will, of course need to position the sensor so that it will be rained upon. Connect the sensor to the Arduino using long cables that pass outside through a window or opening so that the Arduino itself operates in a typical domestic environment and away from moisture which could eventually damage the board.

This sketch again makes use of an 'if' statement to compare the input voltage with the threshold level.

```
/ Rain_alarm.ino

#define AlarmLED 13
#define speaker 9

int ADC_value;
int ADC_0=0;
int threshold = 300;

void setup()
{ Serial.begin(9600);
```

```
    pinMode(AlarmLED, OUTPUT);
  }

  void loop()
  { ADC_value=analogRead(ADC_0);
    Serial.println(ADC_value);

    if(ADC_value > threshold)
      { digitalWrite(AlarmLED,HIGH);
        tone(speaker,1000,100);
        Serial.println("Rain alert!");
      }
    else digitalWrite(AlarmLED,LOW);
    delay(300);
  }
```

NB: Unfortunately, the rain sensor is not 100% stable long-term. In practice, it was found that the sensing elements corrode quite quickly. The sensor then becomes unusable in a comparatively short time.

This particular project is ideal for experimentation purposes but because of the shortcomings of the sensing element it's not suitable for long term operation. Professional sensor units are available from specialist retailers which give better reliability for continuous operation. Their mode of operation is usually the same as the sensor module used here but the conductor tracks are made of a special material. They are of course more expensive but offer better reliability.

Chapter 6 • Motors and Servos control the world

Stepper motors are much more versatile than standard DC motors. Their stator and with it the axle, can be rotated very precisely which makes them ideal for electromechanical-control applications. They are also widely used in the field of robotics.
The technique required to control a stepper motor (also just known as 'steppers'), however is much more complex than for a simple DC motor. Unlike a DC motor, stepping motors have at least four connections. The number of connections depends on the design. There are basically two main types of motor:

- Bipolar motors
- Unipolar motors

Unipolar motors usually have six connections. Their internal structure is more complex than bipolar motors so for the sake of simplicity we will restrict our study to bipolar motors only. Bipolar stepper motors use two independent coils, each having two connections. This gives us the four connections we associate with bipolar motors. The motor included in the kit has four connections so it must also be a bipolar type stepper motor. The diagram below shows the internal arrangement of the motor.

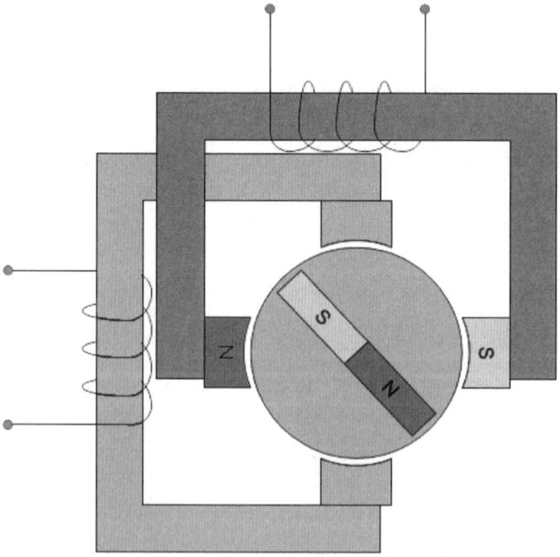

Illustration 72: Bipolar stepper motor basics

To make the motor turn one coil after another is energized. This is made in sequence to produce a rotating field which the magnetic stator in the centre follows. The electrical switching required to produce this rotating field can be easily generated by a microcontroller.

The amount of current that an Arduino port pin can handle is not enough to drive the motor coils directly. The maximum amount of current that each pin can source or sink is 40 mA. The stepper motor coils operate with a current of several hundred milliamps so it's necessary to use a driver chip in between the Arduino and the stepper motor coils to handle the extra current required. A common device used in this type of application is the ULN2003 APG driver chip. This chip can also be found in the motor-driver module in the hardware kit. To make the stepper motor stator turn the microcontroller must output a sequence of 4-bit codes to produce the rotating field. The required signal sequence looks like this where the letters refer to the state of the four outputs connected to the coils.

Step	A	B	C	D
1	1	0	1	0
2	0	1	1	0
3	0	1	0	1
4	1	0	0	1

Each time the four outputs change state the stepper motor rotates by one step. When the sequence is included in a continuous software loop the motor spins continuously. The loop index value will then indicate the number of steps. This technique can be used to determine how far a stepping motor rotates with high precision. Since the number of steps for a full revolution is known, it makes it also possible to calculate how many steps a program loop must execute in order to achieve a certain number of motor revolutions.
A stepper motor will only rotate at the point the bit pattern changes, in between changes the stator is held in position by the magnetic forces generated by the coils according to the last bit sequence.

6.1 The Stepper Motor and Motor Driver Module

The stepping motor included in the hardware kit is particularly suited for use with the Arduino system. It can even operate at the same voltage level used by the Arduino so will not require a separate power supply. The stepper motor plugs directly into the motor control board. This supplies the motor with sufficient current. The power for the motor is provided by the module so the digital pins of the Arduino only supply digital switching signals. The plug on the stepper motor just connects to the matching socket on the module. The plug shape ensures that it can't be plugged in incorrectly.
The following table shows the connections between the motor driver module and the Arduino.

Arduino pin	Module pin	Comments
5V	'+'	External supply can be up to 12 V max.
GND	'-'	External ground
D02	IN4	
D03	IN2	
D04	IN3	
D05	IN1	

NB: Please make sure you use the correct pin assignments otherwise the motor will not operate as intended!

The motor develops high torque even with a 5 V supply. This is because of the built-in gearbox in the stepping motor metal housing. By running it from a higher voltage, the motor power can be increased even further. A maximum of 12 volts may be applied to the driver module's '+' and '-' terminals.

The gearbox also gives the motor very fine motor steps. With this motor one full revolution of the output drive shaft is divided into 2048 individual steps of the motor. This however also has a disadvantage because we can only achieve a relatively low maximum rotational speed.

Illustration 73: The stepper motor driver module

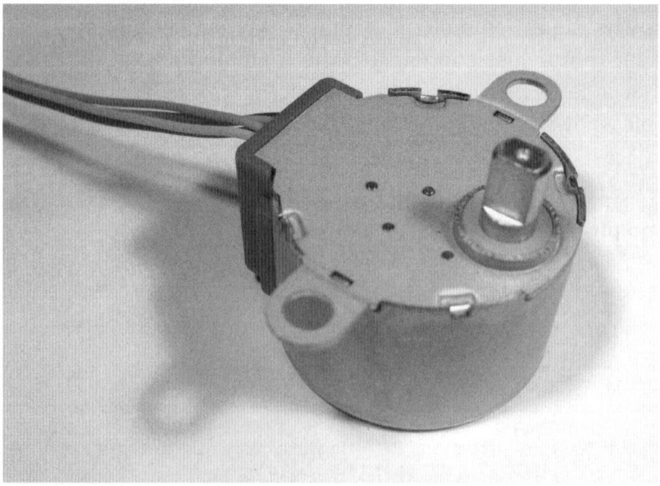

Illustration 74: The stepper motor

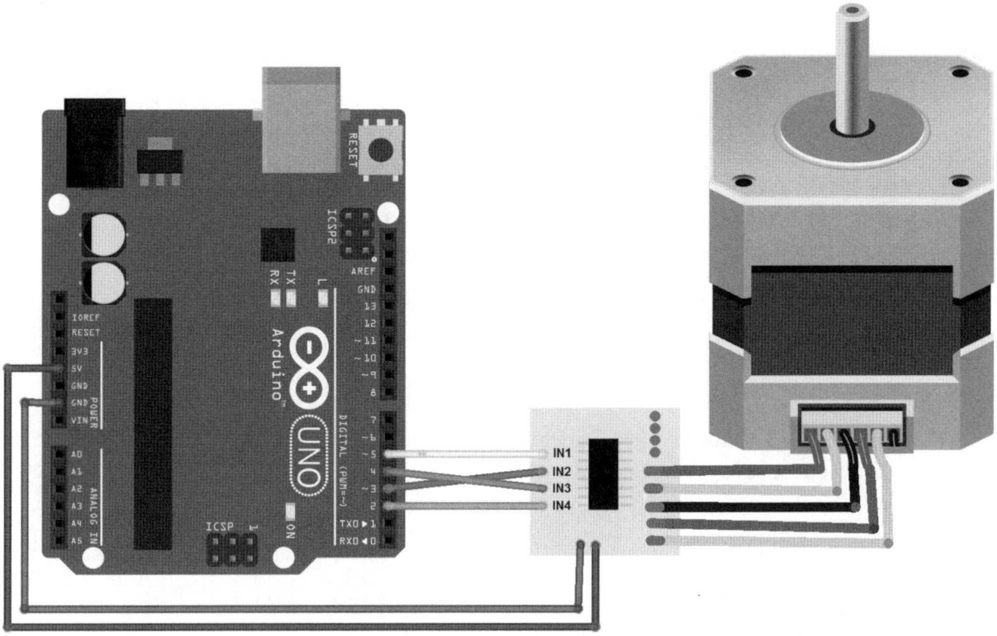

Illustration 75: Hook up between the stepper motor and Arduino

In this first example sketch it makes the motor output shaft turn exactly 2048 steps in one direction and then 2048 steps in the reverse direction. This should convince you that there are in fact 2048 steps in one complete turn of the output shaft for this motor/gearbox combination.

```
// Stepper_test.ino

#include <Stepper.h>
const int stepsPerRev = 32;
Stepper myStepper(stepsPerRev, 2, 3, 4, 5);
void setup()
{ myStepper.setSpeed(500);
}
void loop()
{ myStepper.step(2048);
  delay(500);
  myStepper.step(-2048);
  delay(500);
}
```

6.2 From rotation to single steps

Simple DC electric motors cannot be controlled very precisely. Anyone with a model train set is sure to be aware of this. Running at full speed is no problem but when you try to move the carriages slowly it's difficult to avoid jerky movements and engine stalls. Stepper motors however can operate relatively smoothly at very low rotational speeds. The following sketch demonstrates the various speed ranges possible with this stepper motor:

```
// Stepper_speed.ino

#include <Stepper.h>
const int stepsPerRev = 32;
Stepper myStepper(stepsPerRev, 2, 3, 4, 5);
int motorSpeed;

void setup() {}

void loop()
{ motorSpeed = 1000;    // Range: 1...1000 - slow...fast
  myStepper.setSpeed(motorSpeed);
  myStepper.step(2048);
  delay(500);

  motorSpeed = 300;     // Range: 1...1000 - slow...fast
  myStepper.setSpeed(motorSpeed);
  myStepper.step(2048);
  delay(500);

  motorSpeed = 10;      // Range: 1...1000 - slow...fast
  myStepper.setSpeed(motorSpeed);
  myStepper.step(30);
  delay(500);

  motorSpeed = 1;       // Range: 1...1000 - slow...fast
  myStepper.setSpeed(motorSpeed);
  myStepper.step(10);
  delay(500);
}
```

The engine starts at maximum speed and performs a full revolution. Then the speed is reduced down to about one third. The decrease in speed is clearly visible.
In the third part the speed of the output shaft is reduced to around 100th of its maximum speed. The shaft now rotates at about the same speed as the second hand of a watch. The LEDs are lit to show how the motor coils are driven.

In the last operational mode the sketch reduces the motor speed down by a factor of 10 again so that now the movement of the shaft is hardly noticeable. Nevertheless the motor is moving precisely one step at a time and the LEDs light up to show how the coils are driven.

6.3 Turntable to display Jewelry or scale models

One practical application of a slowly revolving stepper motor is shown below:

Illustration 76: Display turntable

To make the turntable a potentiometer control knob is fitted to the output shaft of the stepper motor and then a round black plastic disk is attached to the knob. This now makes a display platform which could be used to exhibit articles of jewelry, scale models or exhibition items.

The turntable rotating at a suitable speed allows every aspect of the displayed item to be viewed. Halogen spotlighting will also add to the display and produce a very effective presentation.

6.4 Use the Joystick for Motor Control

The joystick can be used to give precise control of the stepper motor.

```
// Stepper_w_joystic_control.ino

#include <Stepper.h>

const int stepsPerRev = 32;
Stepper myStepper(stepsPerRev, 2, 3, 4, 5);

int sensor;
int motorSpeed;

void setup() {}
```

```
void loop()
{ sensor = analogRead(A0);
  motorSpeed = map(sensor, 0, 1023, -1000, 1000);
  if(motorSpeed > 0)
  { myStepper.setSpeed(motorSpeed);
    myStepper.step(1);
  }
  if(motorSpeed < 0)
  { myStepper.setSpeed(-motorSpeed);
    myStepper.step(-1);
  }
}
```

6.5 The Servo as a Universal Actuator

Along with stepper motors the servo can be used to provide precise control of mechanical mechanisms. Like stepper motors, servos also contain a motor and a gearbox but they have an entirely different operational principle.

The servo is made up of a simple DC motor, a potentiometer and an electronic control unit. The potentiometer is attached to the servos output shaft and provides positional information back to the electronic control unit. The electronic control unit continually compares the servo's input control signal to the positional information and makes corrections by rotating the output shaft to minimize any error. This is an example of a control loop and gives very precise control of the servo output shaft.

Servos are widely used in scale model building. Practically every remote controlled aircraft, ship or car uses servos to provide directional control. Servos are also extensively used in the field of robotics.

6.6 Controlled Motor Power: The Servo

General purpose model-makers servos are controlled by a standard control signal. This signal is a special case of **P**ulse **W**idth **M**odulation (PWM) control. It consists of a single pulse sent repeatedly to the servo; the width of this pulse defines the position of the servo ouput arm.

The pulse is sent to the servo at a rate of about 50 times a second or 50 Hertz. This means that the time between each pulse is 20 ms but this timing is not critical because it plays no part in the servo control.

Illustration 77: A Servo

The control information is provided by the width of the pulse. The pulse can have a minimum width of 1 ms and a maximum width of 2 ms. These pulse widths correspond to the maximum and minimum position of the servo output arm. A pulse width of 1.5 ms will position the output arm midway or in its central postion. Although this describes the accepted standard protocol, some manufacturers use slightly different timings and pulse widths. In this case it will be necessary to adapt the control signal accordingly.

The servo rotation direction can also be manufacturer dependant. Some rotate clockwise as the pulse gets narrower while others rotate anticlockwise.

The illustration below shows the servo output arm position and the corresponding contol signal pulse width.

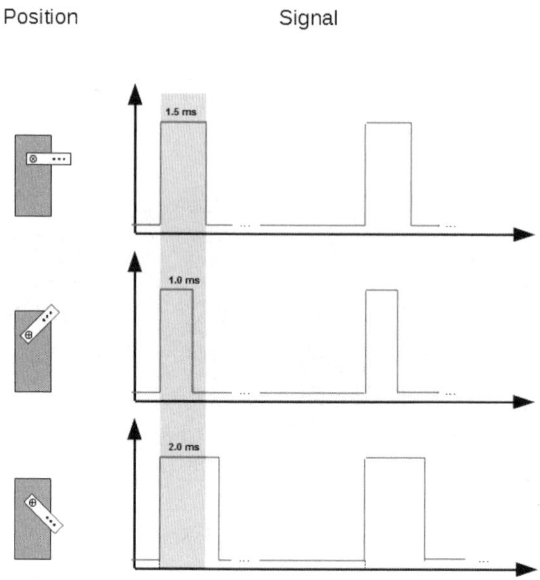

Illustration 78: Servo control signal and arm position

Ideally the servo should have its own power supply. In this case make sure the earth connection for both the Arduino supply and the servo supply are electrically connected together.

When then servo uses the same power supply as the Arduino it can sometimes cause erratic behavior. The servo may draw exececessive current which can cause the supply voltage level to drop momentarily causing the Arduino to reset or malfunction. Sometimes the power supply may not be able to provide enough current for both the servo and Arduino, this can cause the servo arm to shudder or move to its extreme ends. This is less of a problem for small servos like the one included in the kit which will usually be able to operate from the same supply as the Arduino without problem.

Standard servos usually observe the wiring color system shown below:

Connection	**Wire color**
GND	brown or black
Positive supply (usually +5V to +6V)	red
Signal	Orange or white (maybe another color)

Make sure that a servo is never driven beyond its designed operating range. This is usually +/- 45° of its central position. The servo can be damaged if you try to operate it outside these limits.

6.7 The Servo Library

Using routines from the Servo library makes it easy to operate more than one servo from one Arduino board. The library also includes many other useful functions, it will just be necessary first to include the library in the sketch with:

```
#include <Servo.h>
```

Then just with the statement

```
Servo myservo;
```

A new servo object is created and with

```
myservo.attach(PIN);
```

the servo output signal is assigned to a pin number on the Arduino. Now you can use

```
myservo.write(ServoPos);
```

to move the servo arm to a defined position 'ServoPos'. The value for ServoPos can be in the range between 0 and 180. To reduce the risk of damaging the mechanism of some servos you should however only use values between 45 and 135.

Here we can see what the control signal looks like:

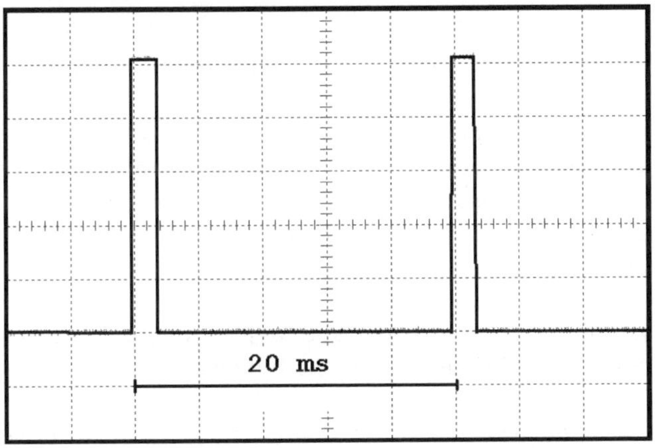

Illustration 79: The servo control signal waveform shown on an oscilloscope

6.8 Precise Servo Control

Just as we used a joystick to control the stepper motor we can also use it to control a servo. This time it's not the rotation speed we will be changing but the position of the servo's output arm.

This is how the joystick and servo are connected to the Arduino board. It may be necessary to supply the servo from a separate supply to avoid loading the Arduino supply. Make sure the ground connection (GND) of the seperate supply is linked to the GND connection on the Arduino.

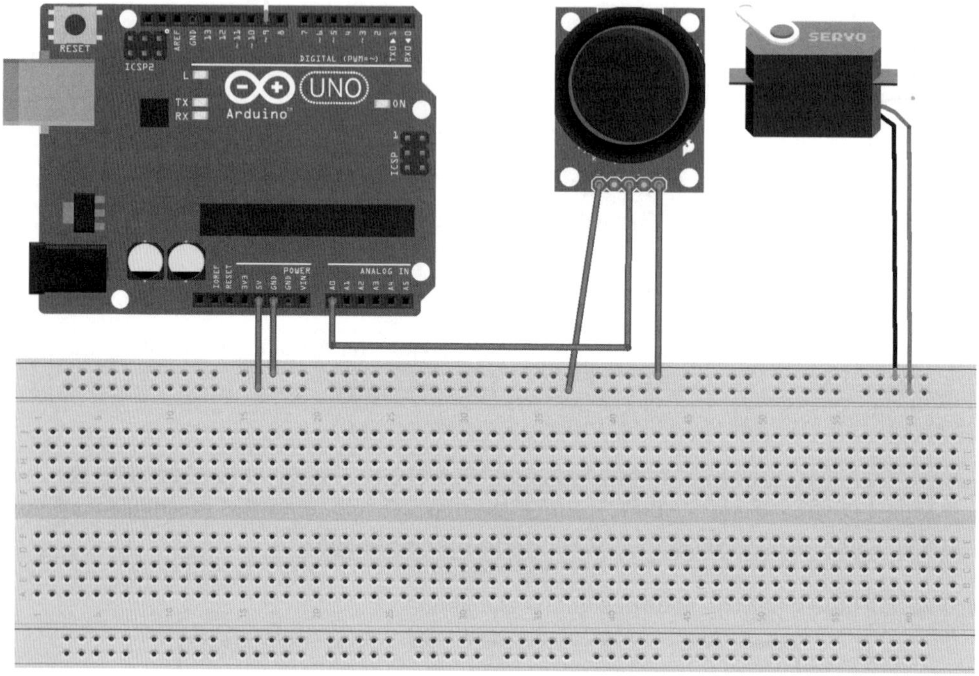

Illustration 80: Using a joystick to control the servo

In principle, this control mechanism corresponds exactly to the mode of operation of a model remote control system; the only thing missing is the radio link between the joystick and servo. You could of course install a radio link using off-the-shelf 433 MHz radio modules for example. For simplicity we can just use long cables to provide the remote control of something like a robot arm.

In the sketch the joystick position is read first at analog input A0. The value is then scaled (to keep it in the range 45 - 135) using the map function:

```
analogVal = map(analogVal, 0, 1023, 45, 135);  // scale servo to 0 and 180
degrees
```

the servo then moves to the position according to the scaled value.

```
// Servo_control_via_joystick.ino

#include <Servo.h>
```

```
Servo myservo;

int analogVal;

void setup() {
  myservo.attach(9);    // servo is connected to Arduino Pin D9
}

void loop() {
  analogVal = analogRead(0);         // joystick is connected to A0
  analogVal = map(analogVal, 0, 1023, 45, 135);  // scale servo to 0 and 180
degrees
  myservo.write(analogVal);
  delay(10);
}
```

In chapter 8.8 a servo will be used as part of a secure door-entry system.

Chapter 7 • Banish the Spaghetti: Control Wirelessly

Without doubt one of the most important technologies of today's world is the wireless transmission of signals. Without any visible link, signals can be transmitted over thousands of kilometers. In modern space technology, radio signals even span distances of millions of kilometers. Apart from the use of the radio spectrum, we can also use light signals to transmit information.

In this chapter we go on to investigate both technologies. First signals are sent using invisible infra-red light. This medium is then used here to control ports on the Arduino.

Then we use the RFID module to show how data can be read from a security tag using radio frequency waves. This type of near-field communication is becoming increasingly important in everyday life. From wireless security cards to remotely readable ID tags, we are becoming more reliant on this technology to keep our personal details safe. It is fascinating to learn more about how this technology works.

7.1 For Convenience: Remote Control with an IR Receiver

We have already used a type of IR detector in a flame detector circuit. However, the Arduino can also be remotely controlled via IR commands. In this case, sequences of signals in the form of infrared light are transmitted from a hand-held remote transmitter to a receiver module attached to the Arduino. Here too the signals are not in the visible spectrum.

You may not be able to see them but any digital camera like the one on your smartphone, for instance has an image sensor with a much wider optical bandwidth and is sensitive to IR signals. This is a good way to test your TV remote to see if the batteries are dead. Point it at your camera lens and press a button, you will be able to see on your camera or smartphone screen the LED on the front of the remote controller flashing. The IR LED is flickering because it's sending out a message which contains information on which key you are pressing. The IR receiver (in the TV) converts the flashing sequence into electrical signals which are then decoded. These coded sequences from the hand-held remote controller can also be easily decoded by the Arduino.

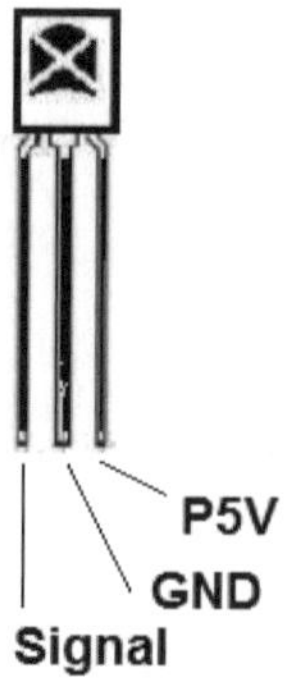

Illustration 81: IR receiver pinouts

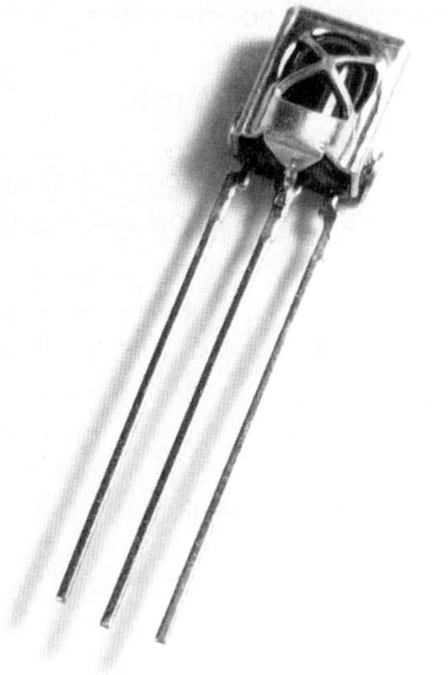

Illustration 82: The IR receiver

Connections between the Arduino and IR receiver module are given in the table:

IR receiver pin	**Arduino pin**
P5V	5V
GND	GND
Signal	D2

The couch potato's friend; the IR remote controller transmitter:

Illustration 83: Hand-held IR remote controller

A library of routines which we need to decode the signals is available at

https://github.com/shirriff/Arduino-IRremote

where it can be downloaded and incorporated into the Arduino IDE libraries. Thanks to the library routines, this next sketch is really very short but it's a good start to quickly test out wireless information transmission.

```
// IR_remote_control_test.ino

#include <IRremote.h>

int RECV_PIN = 2; //ir receiver @ pin2

IRrecv irrecv(RECV_PIN);

decode_results results;

void setup()
{ Serial.begin(9600);
  irrecv.enableIRIn(); // Start the receiver
}

void loop()
{ if (irrecv.decode(&results))
  { Serial.println(results.value, HEX);
    irrecv.resume(); // Receive the next value
  }
  delay(100);
}
```

Pressing button '1' in the remote controller shows the number sequence '16724175' in the serial monitor window. This is the number sequence identifying pushbutton 1. All the other keys also have a sequence associated with them which you can discover by pressing the key.

When you press and hold a key the code sequence '4294967295' is eventually received. This code just identifies that a key is held down; any key generates this code when it's pressed continuously.

This table gives the main characteristics of the IR receiver chip:

Supply voltage	**2.7 V to 5.5 V**
Carrier frequency	37.9 kHz
Acceptance angle	90 ° approx.

The message contains the data as a coded bit sequence. If you have an oscilloscope handy you can put the probe on the output pin of the IR receiver and view the digital messages sent when a key is pressed. The following waveform shows an example of such a bit sequence.

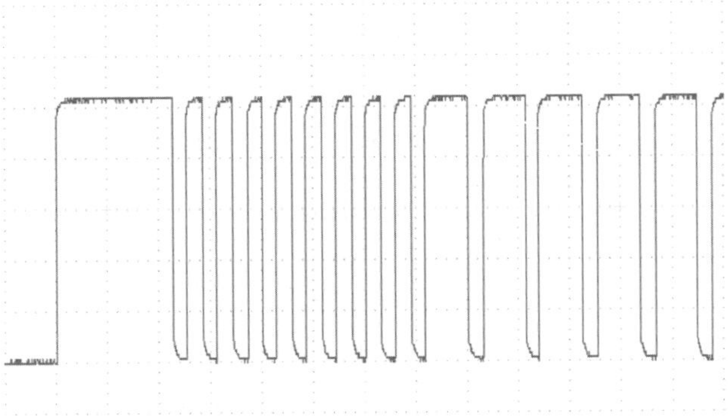

Illustration 84: Signal bit-sequence received by the IR receiver chip

7.2 A Remotely Contolled LED

With the help of the library routines we can now turn the Arduino into a real remote control receiver unit. It's only necessary to check all the received codes and use them to trigger desired events.

The simplest event we could perform here is to turn an LED on and off. It can be arranged that when

- button '1' is pressed: LED is switched on
- button '0' is pressed: LED is switched off

The previous program can be expanded to achieve this control.

```
//  IR_remote_control_LED.ino

#include <IRremote.h>
const int irReceiverPin = 2;  //ir receiver @ pin2
const int ledPin = 13;

IRrecv irrecv(irReceiverPin);
decode_results results;

void setup()
{ pinMode(ledPin,OUTPUT);
  Serial.begin(9600);
  irrecv.enableIRIn();
}

void loop()
```

```
{ if (irrecv.decode(&results))
  { Serial.print("irCode: "); Serial.println(results.value, HEX);
    irrecv.resume();
    delay(100);
    if(results.value == 0x9716BE3F) // key code "1"
    { digitalWrite(ledPin,HIGH);
    Serial.println("key code 1 detected");
    }
    if(results.value == 0xC101E57B) // key code "0"
    { digitalWrite(ledPin,LOW);
      Serial.println("key code 0 detected");
    }
  }
}
```

The codes assigned by manufacturers to the keys are changed quite often. When the sketch isn't working as you would expect you can check the hex value of each key code output on the serial monitor. All you need to do is change the key codes in the sketch to those you see on the serial monitor. Edit the hex code in the lines

```
if(results.value == 0x9716BE3F) // key code "1"
```

and

```
if(results.value == 0xC101E57B) // key code "0"
```

7.3 Wireless Data Reading: The RFID module

RFID reader devices are used to read RFID (**R**adio-**F**requency **ID**entification) tags. The tags can be integrated into items such as credit card-sized cards and key fobs and they are passive in that they have no independant power source. Each tag contains its own unique identification number which can be read by an RF signal. This feature makes them ideal for projects such as an Arduino-based door entry or similar system where the tag is read and identified.

The tags can be encapsulated in different outlines. The following illustrations show the RFID reader module and two RFID tags supplied with the hardware kit. One tag is in a key fob, the other in a plastic credit card format.

The function of the RFID system is based on small transponders. The RFID reader module includes a transmitter that sends out an RF signal which is received by an aerial in the tag. When the tag is close enough, the energy from this signal is enough to power up the tag and it then transmits its information at a fixed frequency which can be read by the reader module. Because the RFID tag is powered by energy from the transmission field, it does not need its own power source. It therefore has no battery and is permanently ready for operation.

The tags contain a memory area where you can write information and read it back. There are also some special types of tag that allow you to allocate a UID. Use of these features are outside the scope of this book, for our applications here we will just read the UIDs stored in the tags.

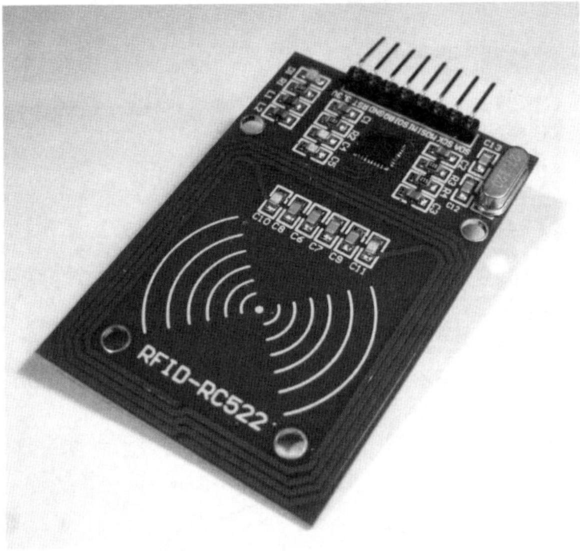

Illustration 85: The RFID Module

Illustration 86: RFID card and key fob

In addition to the tags that we've included with the kit they are also found imbedded in sticky labels inside books and magazines. The information contained in the tag can also be read out using the RFID receiver of the hardware kit.

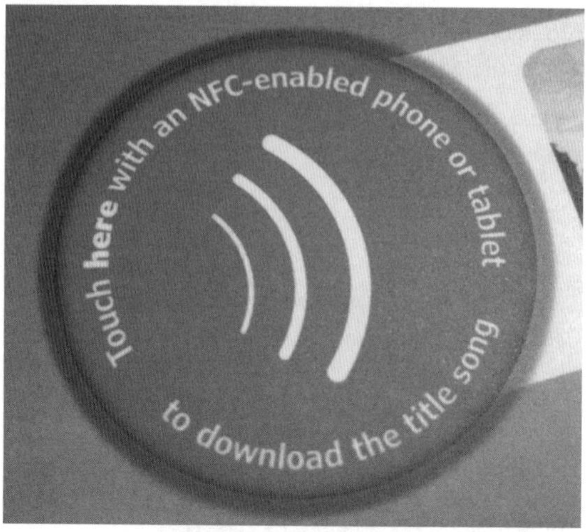

Illustration 87: The RFID tag contains Information

Illustration 88: An RFID tag as a label stuck inside a book

To read data out from the RFID module requires a comparatively high level of programming effort. Thankfully, a ready made library comes to the resue here again. The library is available from:

https://github.com/miguelbalboa/rfid

In this first exercise you will be able to read out the so-called UID or 'Unique IDentifier', which is the unique number programmed into the tag during manufacture. The program looks like this:

```
// RFID-RC522_UID.ino

#include <SPI.h>
#include <MFRC522.h>

// RC522        Arduino UNO
// Pin          Pin
// ---------------------------------------
// RST          9
// SDA(SS)      10
// MOSI         11
// MISO         12
// SCK          13

#define RST_PIN 9
#define SS_PIN 10

MFRC522 mfrc522(SS_PIN, RST_PIN);

void setup()
{ Serial.begin(9600);
  SPI.begin();
  mfrc522.PCD_Init();
  Serial.println("Place RFID TAG in range!");
  delay(300);
}

void loop()
{ // Card present?
  if ( ! mfrc522.PICC_IsNewCardPresent())
  { return;
  }
  // Select card
  if ( ! mfrc522.PICC_ReadCardSerial())
  { return;
  }

  Serial.print("UID of RFID TAGS: ");
  for (byte i = 0; i < mfrc522.uid.size; i++)
  { Serial.print(mfrc522.uid.uidByte[i], HEX);
    Serial.print(" ");
  }
  Serial.println();
}
```

Once you have the program up and running place an RFID tag over the coil of the RFID reader module. The serial monitor will then output the following information:

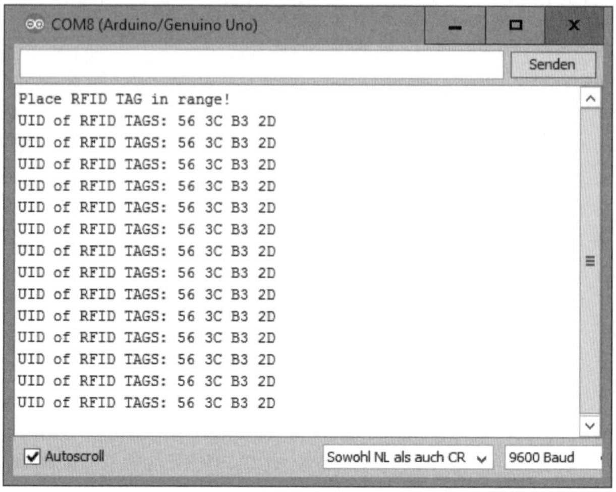

Illustration 89: ID number of an RFID tag

7.4 Contactless door entry control

One of the most important applications of RFID systems is to provide access control. Any person authorized to enter a certain room has their own tag embedded in an ID card, a key fob or in some other form. An RFID reader module positioned at the entrance to the room will open the door locking mechanism when a valid tag comes into range.

Compared to more traditional security-key entry systems the RFID-based system has a number of advantages:

1. When a tag gets lost, it's simple just to delete its UID from the list of authorized tags. Replacement of mechanical lock system and re-issuing of keys is not necessary.

2. A tag costs much less than a security key blank.

3. In a large building installation with multiple door-entry points, individual tags can be selectively excluded from high security areas.

To recognize a particular tag it simplifies calculations if the hex UID value is first converted into a decimal number. This makes it easier to compare the tag number but has the disadvantage is does not check the entire four hex blocks that make up the UID. It would of course be more secure if every individual block was evaluated but this would significantly increase the sketch complexity. To achieve maximum security it will therefore be necessary to modify the sketch.

The following sketch uses a simplified procedure, which should be sufficient for the majority of applications:

```
// RFID-RC522_Code.ino

#include <SPI.h>
#include <MFRC522.h>

// RC522          Arduino UNO
// Pin            Pin
// ---------------------------------------
// RST            9
// SDA(SS)        10
// MOSI           11
// MISO           12
// SCK            13

#define RST_PIN 9
#define SS_PIN 10

MFRC522 mfrc522(SS_PIN, RST_PIN);

long code = 0;
long validCode = 123456;  // enter valid code
int activePin = 7;

void setup()
{ pinMode (activePin, OUTPUT);
  Serial.begin(9600);
  SPI.begin();
  mfrc522.PCD_Init();
  Serial.println("Place RFID TAG in range!");
  delay(300);
}

void loop()
{ // Card present?
  if ( ! mfrc522.PICC_IsNewCardPresent())
  { return;
  }
  // Select card
  if ( ! mfrc522.PICC_ReadCardSerial())
  { return;
  }

  Serial.print("UID of RFID TAGS: ");
  for (byte i = 0; i < mfrc522.uid.size; i++)
  { Serial.print(mfrc522.uid.uidByte[i], HEX);
    Serial.print(" ");
```

```
    }
    Serial.println();

    long code=0;
    for (byte i = 0; i < mfrc522.uid.size; i++)
    {code=((code+mfrc522.uid.uidByte[i])*10);
    }
    Serial.print("Code is: ");
    Serial.println(code);
    if (code == validCode)
    { // valid card detected
       Serial.println("Valid ID detected - activate lock!");
       Serial.println();
       digitalWrite (activePin, HIGH);
       delay (3000);
       digitalWrite (activePin, LOW);
    }
  }
```

With the sketch loaded and running you will now be able to read the code numbers of different TAGs on the serial monitor as you swipe them on the reader module. Write down the code of the tag, which you want as 'authorized access'. Now enter that code sequence in the sketch:

```
  long validCode = 123456;  // enter valid code
```

Once the code has been changed, the sketch can be uploaded. In this example the holder of the tag with the UID 123456 will be allowed access.

When the valid tag is placed within range of the reader module the LED connected to port 7 will be lit for three seconds. In a practical application this signal can also be used to operate an electrical door bolt. Use the serial monitor display to read when the tag has been detected to open the door.

For all other tags no action will be triggered.
In case of emergency or power failure make sure there is always a manual override allowing occupants to quickly exit a building fitted with an electrical door entry system.

7.5 RFID Tags Store Data
In addition to its UID, a relatively large amount of data can also be stored on an RFID tag. The RFID module can also read out this data. The following program reads this data and sends it to the serial interface.

One application of RFID tags is, for example, to store Internet addresses. The tags can be produced very cheaply and widely distributed. They can be incorporated into sticky labels attached to products or books. Using an RFID module or NFC-enabled smart device the label can be scanned and a browser running on the smart device will be directed automatically to the address contained in the label tag without the need to type the address.

The following sketch shows how this information can be read.

```
// RFID-RC522_data.ino

#include <SPI.h>
#include <MFRC522.h>

// RC522          Arduino UNO
// Pin            Pin
// ---------------------------------------
// RST            9
// SDA(SS)        10
// MOSI           11
// MISO           12
// SCK            13

#define RST_PIN          9
#define SS_PIN           10

MFRC522 mfrc522(SS_PIN, RST_PIN);

void setup()
{ Serial.begin(9600);
  SPI.begin();            // Start SPI bus
  mfrc522.PCD_Init();      // Init MFRC522 Reader
  mfrc522.PCD_DumpVersionToSerial();  // Show RC522 details
  Serial.println("Place RFID TAG in range!");
}

void loop()
{ // Card present?
   if ( ! mfrc522.PICC_IsNewCardPresent())
   { return;
   }
  // Select card
  if ( ! mfrc522.PICC_ReadCardSerial())
  { return;
  }

  // Send data to serial
  mfrc522.PICC_DumpToSerial(&(mfrc522.uid));
}
```

Place an RFID close to the reader and you will be able to read the information stored on the tag displayed on the serial monitor. You will need to hold the tag in range during the entire read sequence.

Chapter 8 • Experimental projects for Advanced Users

Following on from the previous projects which were simpler applications using individual modules and components we now present in these last sections, more complex devices and projects.
These projects typically use several modules combined together so that to start off a real-time module with an LCD builds a really practical digital clock.

We have used some of the components before but the applications here will be more complex such as a running text display or implementing a familiar computer game.
Finally we get to build a controller for halogen lights using a relay module and then a complete door-entry system for a room or cupboard with a keypad to enter the access code.

The projects worked through here are of course just the tip of the iceberg. Using the components supplied with the kit you can build a whole host of useful devices. After working through the projects in this book you will be familiar with all the individual modules and components and well equipped to start using them for your own applications. Here are just a few suggestions:

- Noise-triggered halogen lamp
- A cat flap with RFID recognition
- Mood lighting controlled by a joy stick
- Automatic room lighting brightness control
- Etc, etc...

8.1 Always the Right Time: The RTC Module

The Arduino has its own 16 MHz crystal on board to provide the processor clock signal, this is accurate enough to use also as a time base for a digital clock without any additional hardware. Whenever power to the system is turned off the clock would however lose the time setting and would need to be reset to the current time on power up. One way round this problem would be to continually power the Arduino using a backup battery but an even simpler solution is to use an RTC (Real Time Clock) module. These modules keep track of the time and date powered by their onboard 3 V coin cell.
The RTC module only needs to be connected to the Arduino to provide a high-quality digital crystal timebase. The accuracy of this timebase is very high; the RTC module uses a special watch crystal, the precision of which is slightly better than a standard 16 Mhz crystal.
The RTC module included in the kit uses the popular DS1302 timer chip. A library of functions for this device can be found at:

https://github.com/msparks/arduino-ds1302

The following table shows the hookup of the five connections between the RTC module and Arduino:

RTC pin	Arduino pin
Vcc	5V or D03
GND	GND or D04
CLK	D05
DAT	D06
RST	D07

Here is then RTC module showing the coin cell:

Illustration 90: The RTC module with 3 V coin cell

In theory the module can be wired to Arduino using male/female jumper leads but in practice the wires can be a source of trouble for data transfers. It's better to keep the connections as short as possible or better still plug the module directly into the header sockets on the Arduino. There are two possible ways this can be achieved as shown in the illustrations below.

You can choose whichever configuration is more suitable for your application. If you need to use the space above the Arduino to make other connections then use the first version. If you want the smallest physical assembly then choose the second version.

Illustration 91: The RTC module and Arduino -Version I

Illustration 92: The RTC module and Arduino -Version II

The two versions must have the pins correctly identified in the sketch. The clock module uses very little power so we can supply it directly from GPIO pins on the Arduino. For version I port pins D03 and D04 are used to supply power to the module. The sketch must therefore set D03 HIGH and D04 LOW in order to power the module correctly.
The module now needs to be setup with the current time and date. This sketch will do the job nicely.

```
DS1302_set_time.ino
```

In the line

```
Time t(2017, 9, 1, 10, 0, 0, Time::kThursday);
```

The current date and time are set up.

```
// DS1302_set_time.ino

#include <stdio.h>
#include <DS1302.h>

const int kCePin   = 7;  // Chip Enable
const int kIoPin   = 6;  // Input/Output
const int kSclkPin = 5;  // Serial Clock

// Create a DS1302 object.
DS1302 rtc(kCePin, kIoPin, kSclkPin);

String dayAsString(const Time::Day day) {
  switch (day) {
    case 1: return "Sunday";
    case 2: return "Monday";
    case 3: return "Tuesday";
    case 4: return "Wednesday";
    case 5: return "Thursday";
    case 6: return "Friday";
    case 7: return "Saturday";
  }
  return "(ERROR)";
}

void printTime()
{ Time t = rtc.time();
  const String day = dayAsString(t.day);
  char buf[50];
  snprintf(buf, sizeof(buf), "%s %04d-%02d-%02d %02d:%02d:%02d",
           day.c_str(),
           t.yr, t.mon, t.date,
           t.hr, t.min, t.sec);
  Serial.println(buf);
}


void setup() {
  Serial.begin(9600);
```

```
  pinMode(3, OUTPUT);  digitalWrite(3, HIGH); // VCC
  pinMode(4, OUTPUT);  digitalWrite(4, LOW);  // GND
  rtc.writeProtect(false);
  rtc.halt(false);
  // Thursday, 7. September, 10:00:00
  Time t(2017, 9, 7, 10, 0, 0, Time::kThursday);
  rtc.time(t);
}

// Loop and print the time every second.
void loop() {
  printTime();
  delay(1000);
}
```

Once the date and time have been entered you can read the module at any time to find the correct time and date as long as the coin cell battery has not died. You will of course need to reenter the date etc when the battery has been replaced.

The following sketch shows how the time and date information is read from the RTC module. Here the information is output to the serial monitor.

```
// DS1302_read_time.ino

#include <stdio.h>
#include <DS1302.h>

// Pins:  RST,DAT,CLK
DS1302 rtc(7, 6, 5);

String dayAsString(const Time::Day day) {
  switch (day) {
    case 1: return "Sunday";
    case 2: return "Monday";
    case 3: return "Tuesday";
    case 4: return "Wednesday";
    case 5: return "Thursday";
    case 6: return "Friday";
    case 7: return "Saturday";
  }
  return "(ERROR)";
}

void printTime()
{ Time t = rtc.time();
  const String day = dayAsString(t.day);
```

```
  char buf[50];
  snprintf(buf, sizeof(buf), "%s %04d-%02d-%02d %02d:%02d:%02d",
           day.c_str(),
           t.yr, t.mon, t.date,
           t.hr, t.min, t.sec);
  Serial.println(buf);
}

void setup()
{ Serial.begin(9600);
  pinMode(3, OUTPUT);  digitalWrite(3, HIGH); // VCC
  pinMode(4, OUTPUT);  digitalWrite(4, LOW);  // GND
}

void loop() {
  printTime();
  delay(1000);
}
```

When the module is plugged in according to version II the pin assignments must be changed to:

```
const int kCePin   = 3;  // Chip Enable
const int kIoPin   = 4;  // Input/Output
const int kSclkPin = 5;  // Serial Clock
```

and to assign the port pins for the supply and ground connections to the module:

```
pinMode(7, OUTPUT);  digitalWrite(7, HIGH); // VCC
pinMode(6, OUTPUT);  digitalWrite(6, LOW);  // GND
```

8.2 Digital clocks and timers for precise time measurements

A real time clock is often an essential element in many microcontroller-based applications. The current time and date in one form or another (particularly with battery retention) are required for systems such as programmable central heating controllers, timeswitches for lighting, automatic blinds etc,.

In its most basic function you can also use it to build a digital clock of your own design. The display could use seven-segment displays or an alphanumeric LCD with the current time and date information also displayed. The following project builds just such a clock using the RTC module and the 16 x 2-line LCD supplied with the kit.

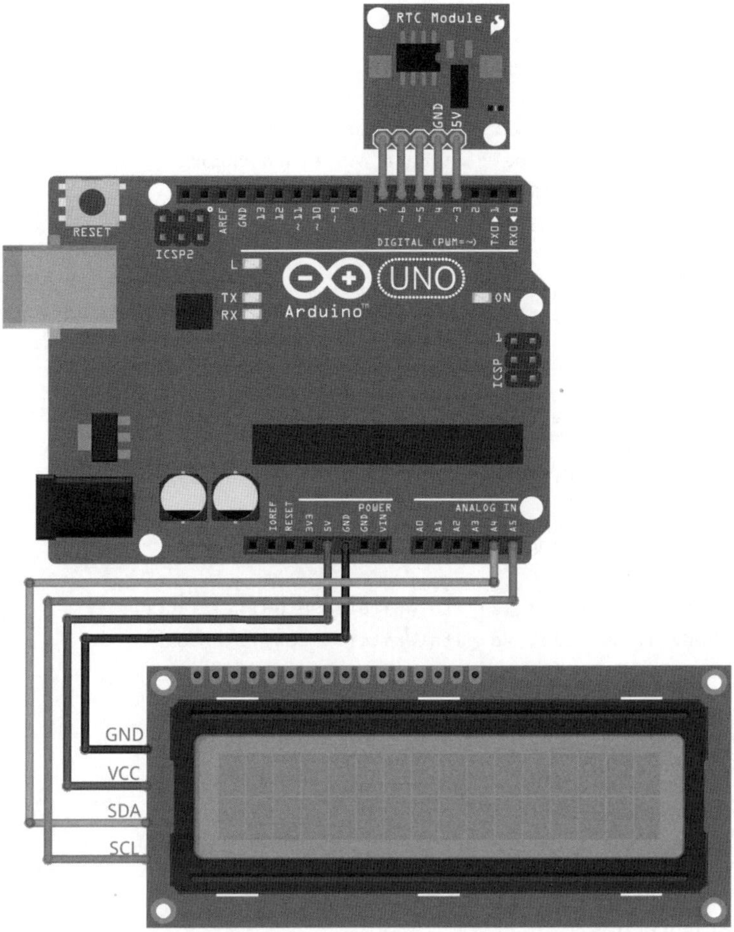

Illustration 93: Digital clock using the RTC module

Using the libraries we have already loaded to the Arduino IDE the complete sketch for the clock is really compact:

```
// DS1302_LCD_clock.ino

#include <stdio.h>
#include <DS1302.h>
#include <Wire.h>
#include <LiquidCrystal_I2C.h>

// Set the LCD address to 0x27 for a 16 chars and 2 line display
LiquidCrystal_I2C lcd(0x27, 16, 2);

// Pins:  RST,DAT,CLK
DS1302 rtc(7, 6, 5);
```

```
String dayAsString(const Time::Day day)
{ switch (day)
  { case 1: return "Sun";    case 2: return "Mon";
    case 3: return "Tue";    case 4: return "Wed";
    case 5: return "Thu";    case 6: return "Fri";
    case 7: return "Sat";
  }
  return "(ERROR)";
}

void setup()
{ // initialize the LCD
  lcd.begin();
  // Turn on the blacklight and print start message
  lcd.backlight();
  lcd.print("Starting Clock!");
  delay(3000);
  pinMode(3, OUTPUT);  digitalWrite(3, HIGH); // VCC
  pinMode(4, OUTPUT);  digitalWrite(4, LOW);  // GND
}

void loop()
{ Time t = rtc.time();
  const String day = dayAsString(t.day);
  char buf1[16];
  snprintf(buf1, sizeof(buf1), " %s, %02d.%02d.%04d", day.c_str(), t.date,
t.mon, t.yr);
  char buf2[16];
  snprintf(buf2, sizeof(buf2), "    %02d:%02d:%02d", t.hr, t.min, t.sec);
  lcd.setCursor(0, 0); lcd.println(buf1);
  lcd.setCursor(15, 0); lcd.println(" ");
  lcd.setCursor(0, 1); lcd.println(buf2);
  lcd.setCursor(12, 1); lcd.println("    ");
  delay(1000);
}
```

Illustration 94: Time and date display

8.3 Conway's Game of Life

Game-playing is one of the most popular applications of computer and microprocessor-based systems. Dating back to the 1970s Conway's 'Game of Life' (or just 'Life') must by now be a classic and has already been implemented on many different computer platforms using various computer languages.

The game was originally developed by the mathematician John H. Conway to represent the behavior of living cell cultures. Individual cells can be represented by LEDs arranged as a matrix. The 8 x 8 LED matrix supplied with this kit is ideal for this application.

The hardware used is connected as in the illustration in 3.17.

The sketch for the game looks like this:

```
// Dot_matrix_LIVE.ino

#include <FrequencyTimer2.h>

byte const MATRIX_SIZE = 8, start_density = 40;
int matPin[16]= {13, 12, 11, 10, 16, 17, 18, 19, 2, 3, 4, 5, 6, 7, 8, 9};
int col[MATRIX_SIZE] = {matPin[12], matPin[2], matPin[3], matPin[9],
matPin[5], matPin[10], matPin[14], matPin[15]};
int row[MATRIX_SIZE] = {matPin[8], matPin[13], matPin[7], matPin[11],
matPin[0], matPin[6], matPin[1], matPin[4]};
// default start condition
byte state[MATRIX_SIZE][MATRIX_SIZE][2] =
           { 1, 0, 1, 0, 1, 0, 0, 0,   1, 0, 1, 0, 1, 0, 1, 0,
             0, 0, 0, 0, 1, 0, 1, 0,   1, 0, 0, 0, 0, 0, 0, 0,
             1, 0, 1, 0, 1, 0, 1, 0,   1, 0, 0, 0, 1, 0, 0, 0,
             0, 0, 0, 0, 0, 0, 1, 0,   1, 0, 0, 0, 0, 0, 1, 0,
             1, 0, 1, 0, 0, 0, 1, 0,   0, 0, 1, 0, 1, 0, 0, 0,
             0, 0, 1, 0, 0, 0, 0, 0,   1, 0, 1, 0, 1, 0, 1, 0,
             0, 0, 1, 0, 1, 0, 1, 0,   0, 0, 1, 0, 1, 0, 0, 0,
            };
byte cells[MATRIX_SIZE][MATRIX_SIZE], cl = 0;

void setup()
{ // initailize and reset matrix
  for (int i = 0; i < 2*MATRIX_SIZE; i++) pinMode(matPin[i], OUTPUT);
  for (int i = 0; i < MATRIX_SIZE; i++)
  { digitalWrite(col[i], HIGH);
    digitalWrite(row[i], HIGH);
  }
  // reset display
  for (int i = 0; i < 8; i++)
    for (int j = 0; j < 8; j++) cells[i][j] = 0;
```

```
  FrequencyTimer2::setPeriod(2000);
  FrequencyTimer2::setOnOverflow(display);
  /*
  // random start condition
  randomSeed(analogRead(0));
  for (int i = 0; i < MATRIX_SIZE; i++)
  {   for (int j = 0; j < MATRIX_SIZE; j++)
      { if (random(100) < start_density) state[i][j][0] = 1;
        else state[i][j][0] = 0;
        state[i][j][1] = 0;
      }
  }
  */
}

void loop() {
  // show state
  for (int i = 0; i < MATRIX_SIZE; i++)
    for (int j = 0; j < MATRIX_SIZE; j++) cells[i][j] = state[i][j][0];
  delay(80);
  // cycles
  for (int x = 0; x < MATRIX_SIZE; x++)
  { for (int y = 0; y < MATRIX_SIZE; y++)
    { state[x][y][1] = state[x][y][0];
      int count = neighbours(x, y);
      if (count == 3 && state[x][y][0] == 0) state[x][y][1] = 1; // cell is
                                                                  // born
      if ((count < 2 || count > 3) && state[x][y][0] == 1) state[x][y][1] =
0;   // cell dies
    }
  }
  // next generation
  for (int x = 0; x < MATRIX_SIZE; x++)
    for (int y = 0; y < MATRIX_SIZE; y++) state[x][y][0] = state[x][y][1];
}

int neighbours(int x, int y)
{ return  state[(x + MATRIX_SIZE - 1) % MATRIX_SIZE][(y + MATRIX_SIZE - 1) %
MATRIX_SIZE][0] +
          state[(x + 1) % MATRIX_SIZE][y][0] + state[x][(y + 1) % MATRIX_
SIZE][0] +
          state[(x + MATRIX_SIZE - 1) % MATRIX_SIZE][(y + 1) % MATRIX_SIZE]
[0] +
          state[(x + 1) % MATRIX_SIZE][(y + MATRIX_SIZE - 1) % MATRIX_SIZE]
[0]+
          state[(x + 1) % MATRIX_SIZE][(y + 1) % MATRIX_SIZE][0] + state[(x
```

```
+ MATRIX_SIZE - 1) % MATRIX_SIZE][y][0] +
          state[x][(y + MATRIX_SIZE - 1) % MATRIX_SIZE][0];
}

void display()  // display refresh
{  digitalWrite(col[cl], HIGH);
   cl++;
   if (cl == MATRIX_SIZE) cl = 0;
   for (int rw = 0; rw < MATRIX_SIZE; rw++)
   {  if (cells[cl][MATRIX_SIZE - 1 - rw] == 1) digitalWrite(row[rw], HIGH);
      else digitalWrite(row[rw], LOW);
   }
   digitalWrite(col[cl], LOW);
}
```

The initial state of the matrix is given by

```
byte state[MATRIX_SIZE][MATRIX_SIZE][2] =
          {  1, 0, 1, 0, 1, 0, 0, 0,   1, 0, 1, 0, 1, 0, 1, 0,
             0, 0, 0, 0, 1, 0, 1, 0,   1, 0, 0, 0, 0, 0, 0, 0,
             1, 0, 1, 0, 1, 0, 1, 0,   1, 0, 0, 0, 1, 0, 0, 0,
             0, 0, 0, 0, 0, 0, 1, 0,   1, 0, 0, 0, 0, 0, 1, 0,
             1, 0, 1, 0, 0, 0, 1, 0,   0, 0, 1, 0, 1, 0, 0, 0,
             0, 0, 1, 0, 0, 0, 0, 0,   1, 0, 1, 0, 1, 0, 1, 0,
             0, 0, 1, 0, 1, 0, 1, 0,   0, 0, 1, 0, 1, 0, 0, 0,
           };
```

Columns 1, 3, 5, ... are active, the others are used for intermediate storage. To change the initial state it's only necessary to vary the active columns.
It's also possible to begin with a random assignment. This code fragment shows how it's done

```
/*
  // random start condition
  randomSeed(analogRead(0));
  for (int i = 0; i < MATRIX_SIZE; i++)
  {   for (int j = 0; j < MATRIX_SIZE; j++)
      { if (random(100) < start_density) state[i][j][0] = 1;
        else state[i][j][0] = 0;
        state[i][j][1] = 0;
      }
  }
*/
```

In the original sketch listing this section has been commented out using /* and */ markers, to use the random assignment it will be necessary to remove both comment markers. The initial pattern will now be different each time the game is rebooted.

8.4 Hello Matrix!

In addition to displaying simple graphics, LED dot-matrix displays are also commonly used to display text characters. Buses and trains use them to show destination information and many are also evident in subway stations and waiting rooms.

This project shows how to display a text message using a single 8 x 8 dot-matrix LED display with each character appearing one after another.

```
// Dot_matrix_HELLO.ino

#include <FrequencyTimer2.h>

#define H { \
    {0, 1, 1, 0, 0, 1, 1, 0}, \
    {0, 1, 1, 0, 0, 1, 1, 0}, \
    {0, 1, 1, 0, 0, 1, 1, 0}, \
    {0, 1, 1, 1, 1, 1, 1, 0}, \
    {0, 1, 1, 1, 1, 1, 1, 0}, \
    {0, 1, 1, 0, 0, 1, 1, 0}, \
    {0, 1, 1, 0, 0, 1, 1, 0}, \
    {0, 1, 1, 0, 0, 1, 1, 0}  \
}

#define E  { \
    {0, 1, 1, 1, 1, 1, 1, 0}, \
    {0, 1, 1, 1, 1, 1, 1, 0}, \
    {0, 1, 1, 0, 0, 0, 0, 0}, \
    {0, 1, 1, 1, 1, 1, 1, 0}, \
    {0, 1, 1, 1, 1, 1, 1, 0}, \
    {0, 1, 1, 0, 0, 0, 0, 0}, \
    {0, 1, 1, 1, 1, 1, 1, 0}, \
    {0, 1, 1, 1, 1, 1, 1, 0}  \
}

#define L { \
    {0, 1, 1, 0, 0, 0, 0, 0}, \
    {0, 1, 1, 0, 0, 0, 0, 0}, \
    {0, 1, 1, 0, 0, 0, 0, 0}, \
    {0, 1, 1, 0, 0, 0, 0, 0}, \
    {0, 1, 1, 0, 0, 0, 0, 0}, \
    {0, 1, 1, 0, 0, 0, 0, 0}, \
    {0, 1, 1, 1, 1, 1, 1, 0}, \
    {0, 1, 1, 1, 1, 1, 1, 0}  \
}
```

```
#define O { \
    {0, 0, 0, 1, 1, 0, 0, 0}, \
    {0, 0, 1, 1, 1, 1, 0, 0}, \
    {0, 1, 1, 0, 0, 1, 1, 0}, \
    {0, 1, 1, 0, 0, 1, 1, 0}, \
    {0, 1, 1, 0, 0, 1, 1, 0}, \
    {0, 1, 1, 0, 0, 1, 1, 0}, \
    {0, 0, 1, 1, 1, 1, 0, 0}, \
    {0, 0, 0, 1, 1, 0, 0, 0}  \
}

#define SPACE { \
    {0, 0, 0, 0, 0, 0, 0, 0}, \
    {0, 0, 0, 0, 0, 0, 0, 0}, \
    {0, 0, 0, 0, 0, 0, 0, 0}, \
    {0, 0, 0, 0, 0, 0, 0, 0}, \
    {0, 0, 0, 0, 0, 0, 0, 0}, \
    {0, 0, 0, 0, 0, 0, 0, 0}, \
    {0, 0, 0, 0, 0, 0, 0, 0}, \
    {0, 0, 0, 0, 0, 0, 0, 0}  \
}
byte column = 0;
byte LEDs[8][8];

int col[8] = {6, 11, 10, 3, 17, 4, 8, 9};
int row[8] =  {2, 7, 19, 5, 13, 18, 12, 16};

const int numPatterns = 5;
byte patterns[numPatterns][8][8] = { H,E,L,L,O };

int pattern = 0;

void setup() {
  // sets the pins as output
  for (int i = 2; i <= 19; i++)
  { pinMode(i, OUTPUT);
  }

  // set up cols and rows
  for (int i = 1; i <= 8; i++)
  { digitalWrite(col[i - 1], HIGH);
  }

  for (int i = 1; i <= 8; i++)
  { digitalWrite(row[i - 1], HIGH);
```

```
    }

    clearLEDs();

    // Turn off toggling of pin 11
    FrequencyTimer2::disable();
    // Set refresh rate (interrupt timeout period)
    FrequencyTimer2::setPeriod(2000);
    // Set interrupt routine to be called
    FrequencyTimer2::setOnOverflow(display);
    setPattern(pattern);
  }

  void loop() {
      pattern = ++pattern % numPatterns;
      setPattern(pattern);
      delay(1000);
      clearLEDs();
      delay(100);
      // slidePattern(pattern, 60);
  }

  void clearLEDs() {
    // Clear display array
    for (int i = 0; i < 8; i++) {
      for (int j = 0; j < 8; j++) {
        LEDs[i][j] = 0;
      }
    }
  }

  void setPattern(int pattern) {
    for (int i = 0; i < 8; i++) {
      for (int j = 0; j < 8; j++) {
        LEDs[i][j] = patterns[pattern][i][j];
      }
    }
  }

  // Interrupt routine
  void display() {
    digitalWrite(col[column], HIGH);  // Turn whole previous column off
    column++;
    if (column == 8) {
      column = 0;
    }
```

```
    for (int r = 0; r < 8; r++) {
      if (LEDs[column][7 - r] == 1) {
        digitalWrite(row[r], HIGH);  // Turn on this led
      }
      else {
        digitalWrite(row[r], LOW); // Turn off this led
      }
    }
    digitalWrite(col[column], LOW); // Turn whole column on at once (for equal
                                    // lighting times)
  }
```

8.5 Live Ticker and Running Text

This project takes the 8 x 8 matrix display one step further by displaying running text, classically used by stock markets around the world to display movements in stock prices. They are also known as 'live stock tickers'. Larger versions are also commonly used to build advertising hoardings surrounding sports events showing continuously changing messages.

```
// Dot_matrix_TICKER.ino

#include <FrequencyTimer2.h>

#define H { \
    {0, 1, 1, 0, 0, 1, 1, 0}, \
    {0, 1, 1, 0, 0, 1, 1, 0}, \
    {0, 1, 1, 0, 0, 1, 1, 0}, \
    {0, 1, 1, 1, 1, 1, 1, 0}, \
    {0, 1, 1, 1, 1, 1, 1, 0}, \
    {0, 1, 1, 0, 0, 1, 1, 0}, \
    {0, 1, 1, 0, 0, 1, 1, 0}, \
    {0, 1, 1, 0, 0, 1, 1, 0}  \
}

#define E  { \
    {0, 1, 1, 1, 1, 1, 1, 0}, \
    {0, 1, 1, 1, 1, 1, 1, 0}, \
    {0, 1, 1, 0, 0, 0, 0, 0}, \
    {0, 1, 1, 1, 1, 1, 1, 0}, \
    {0, 1, 1, 1, 1, 1, 1, 0}, \
    {0, 1, 1, 0, 0, 0, 0, 0}, \
    {0, 1, 1, 1, 1, 1, 1, 0}, \
    {0, 1, 1, 1, 1, 1, 1, 0}  \
}

#define L { \
    {0, 1, 1, 0, 0, 0, 0, 0}, \
```

```
    {0, 1, 1, 0, 0, 0, 0, 0}, \
    {0, 1, 1, 0, 0, 0, 0, 0}, \
    {0, 1, 1, 0, 0, 0, 0, 0}, \
    {0, 1, 1, 0, 0, 0, 0, 0}, \
    {0, 1, 1, 0, 0, 0, 0, 0}, \
    {0, 1, 1, 1, 1, 1, 1, 0}, \
    {0, 1, 1, 1, 1, 1, 1, 0}  \
}

#define O { \
    {0, 0, 0, 1, 1, 0, 0, 0}, \
    {0, 0, 1, 1, 1, 1, 0, 0}, \
    {0, 1, 1, 0, 0, 1, 1, 0}, \
    {0, 1, 1, 0, 0, 1, 1, 0}, \
    {0, 1, 1, 0, 0, 1, 1, 0}, \
    {0, 1, 1, 0, 0, 1, 1, 0}, \
    {0, 0, 1, 1, 1, 1, 0, 0}, \
    {0, 0, 0, 1, 1, 0, 0, 0}  \
}

#define SPACE { \
    {0, 0, 0, 0, 0, 0, 0, 0}, \
    {0, 0, 0, 0, 0, 0, 0, 0}, \
    {0, 0, 0, 0, 0, 0, 0, 0}, \
    {0, 0, 0, 0, 0, 0, 0, 0}, \
    {0, 0, 0, 0, 0, 0, 0, 0}, \
    {0, 0, 0, 0, 0, 0, 0, 0}, \
    {0, 0, 0, 0, 0, 0, 0, 0}, \
    {0, 0, 0, 0, 0, 0, 0, 0}  \
}
byte column = 0;
byte LEDs[8][8];

int col[8] = {6, 11, 10, 3, 17, 4, 8, 9};
int row[8] =  {2, 7, 19, 5, 13, 18, 12, 16};

const int numPatterns = 6;
byte patterns[numPatterns][8][8] = { H,E,L,L,O, SPACE };

int pattern = 0;

void setup() {
  // sets the pins as output
  for (int i = 2; i <= 19; i++)
  { pinMode(i, OUTPUT);
  }
```

```
  // set up cols and rows
  for (int i = 1; i <= 8; i++)
  { digitalWrite(col[i - 1], HIGH);
  }

  for (int i = 1; i <= 8; i++)
  { digitalWrite(row[i - 1], HIGH);
  }

  clearLEDs();

  // Turn off toggling of pin 11
  FrequencyTimer2::disable();
  // Set refresh rate (interrupt timeout period)
  FrequencyTimer2::setPeriod(2000);
  // Set interrupt routine to be called
  FrequencyTimer2::setOnOverflow(display);
  setPattern(pattern);
}

void loop() {
    pattern = ++pattern % numPatterns;
    slidePattern(pattern, 100);
}

void clearLEDs() {
  // Clear display array
  for (int i = 0; i < 8; i++) {
    for (int j = 0; j < 8; j++) {
      LEDs[i][j] = 0;
    }
  }
}

void setPattern(int pattern) {
  for (int i = 0; i < 8; i++) {
    for (int j = 0; j < 8; j++) {
      LEDs[i][j] = patterns[pattern][i][j];
    }
  }
}

void slidePattern(int pattern, int del) {
  for (int l = 0; l < 8; l++) {
    for (int i = 0; i < 7; i++) {
```

```
      for (int j = 0; j < 8; j++) {
        LEDs[j][i] = LEDs[j][i+1];
      }
    }
    for (int j = 0; j < 8; j++) {
     LEDs[j][7] = patterns[pattern][j][0 + l];
    }
    delay(del);
  }
}

// Interrupt routine
void display() {
  digitalWrite(col[column], HIGH);  // Turn whole previous column off
  column++;
  if (column == 8) {
    column = 0;
  }
  for (int r = 0; r < 8; r++) {
    if (LEDs[column][7 - r] == 1) {
      digitalWrite(row[r], HIGH);  // Turn on this led
    }
    else {
      digitalWrite(row[r], LOW); // Turn off this led
    }
  }
  digitalWrite(col[column], LOW); // Turn whole column on at once (for equal
                                  // lighting times)
}
```

8.6 Switching High Power Loads: The Relay Module

In all the applications so far we have only needed to control relatively low power devices. For more ambitious control applications such as home automation projects it will be necessary to switch higher levels of voltage and current.

A relay can be used to switch the power in this sort of application. The relay module included with the kit is approved for switching high voltages but working with a supply voltage greater than 50 V requires special expertise. Please pay attention to the following warning:

WARNING: Working with equipment powered by domestic mains voltage (230 V) can be **lethal** and requires appropriate training. If you are not suitably qualified please do not attempt to work on any project which connects with the mains power supply!

As well as working at higher voltages the relay can also switch up to 10 A current. One interesting use of the relay would be to switch halogen lamps. These can be used very effectively for room lighting and spotlighting. The big advantage of using this type of lamp is that they are powered from 12 V which is generally considered not to be a dangerous voltage to work with.

The relay module has three connections, the table below shows how it is connected to the Arduino:

Relay module	Arduino
+	5V
-	GND
S	D13

Illustration 95: The Relay Module

8.7 Remote controlled Halogen Lamp

The classic low-voltage halogen lamps have a big advantage for users because they operate from a safe 12 V supply. This makes them very flexible as a means of providing room lighting. It is not necessary to take precautions to avoid contact with the wires carrying the 12 V supply; inadvertent contact with the conductors would not normally entail any risk of death or injury. The methods of switching the low voltage supply are also inherently safe and it's a job that can be easily performed by the relay module included in the kit.

The contacts load rating of a relay is usually indicated on its housing. The rating for example could be 10 A maximum at 28 V. This rating would be sufficient to switch a 50 W halogen lamp. It pays to be aware that at this level of current the lamp will be dissipating a lot of this energy as heat and can cause serious burns and will cause a fire if it is operated too close to combustible material!
Once again, be aware of the dangers:

Warning: Halogen lighting systems can present a considerable fire hazard. If you do not have the appropriate expertise in working with high currents and the necessary safety measures, do not install halogen and similar low voltage lighting systems.

From the control point of view however it is relatively easy to handle. The illustration below shows how the IR remote controller included in the kit controls the relay module which interrupts the low voltage supply to the 12 V lamp.

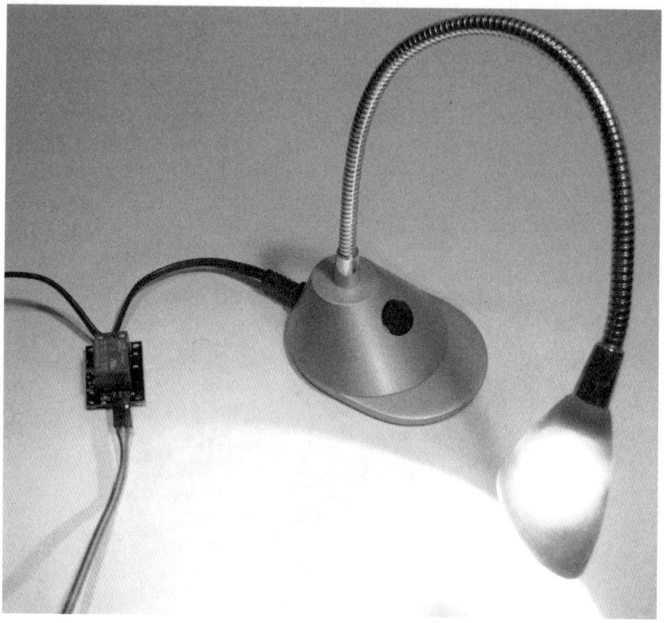

Illustration 96: Relay controlled low voltage halogen lamp

From the software stand point we just use the sketch from chapter 7.2 (Remote controlled LED). Once the program has been loaded the LED13 on the Arduino will light at the same time the relay operates when it is switched by the IR signal from the handheld remote controller.

8.8 Keypad Door Entry System

One important application of electronic systems is in property protection. As well as alarm systems there are also electronic access or door entry control systems. More and more electronic locks used in the private sector as well as in the professional field. It's no longer necessary to fiddle with a bunch of keys to gain access to a secure area; you just need to enter the correct code on a keypad.

This project is a keyless entry system using a keypad as the input device. A servo is used to release a door bolt when the correct key code is entered. In practice you just need to connect up the servo to operate a burglar-resistant bolt. Make sure there is a manual override so that you can quickly exit through any door fitted with an electronic entry system in case of emergency or power failure.

The following Illustration shows how the components are wired up.

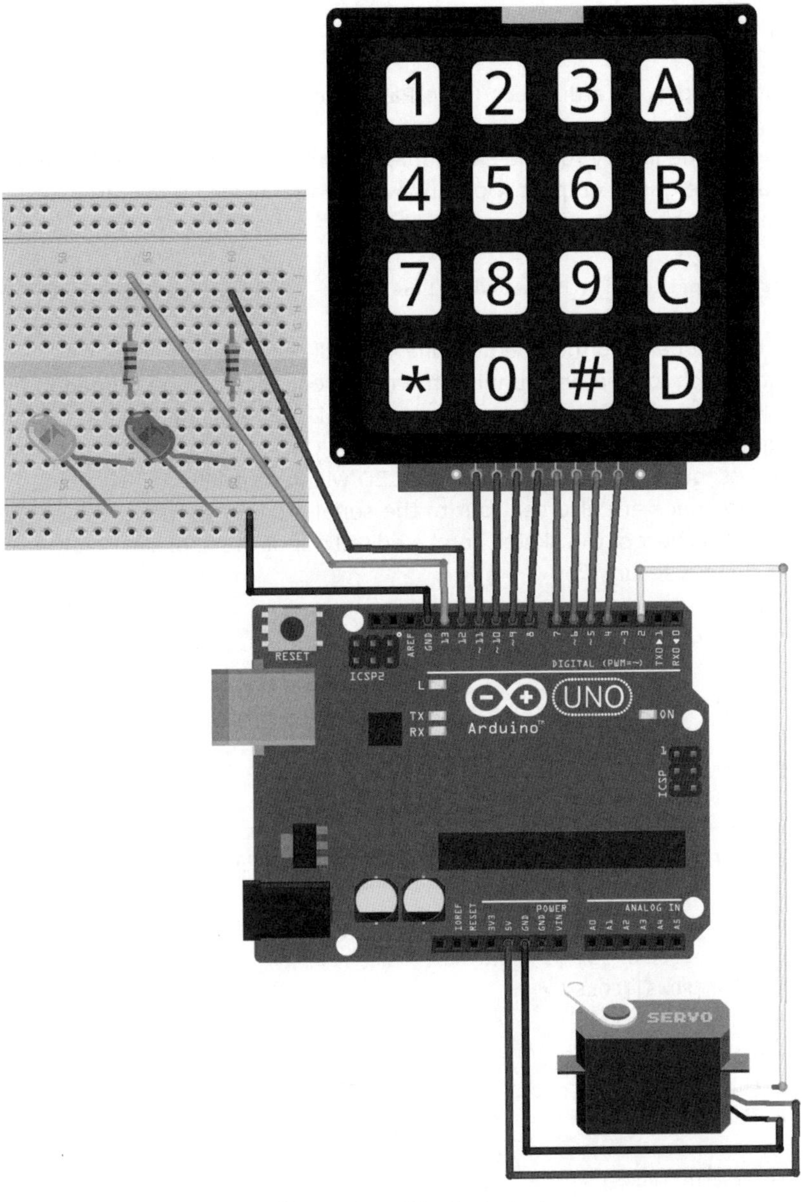

Illustration 97: Code lock

For this sketch we make use of three libraries.

- The Servo library
- The Keypad library
- The Password library

The first two libraries have already been installed in earlier chapters and the Password library can be downloaded at

http://playground.arduino.cc/Code/Password

By making use of the library routines available in the three libraries the sketch for the code lock turns out to be quite compact. Operation of the unit is also straightforward.
Find this line in the sketch

```
Password password = Password( "123456" ); // change password here!
```

And change the sequence of numbers to one you will remember.
Now with the sketch loaded and running the code sequence can be tapped in followed by the 'A' key. When the code is correct the green LED will light and the servo output arm move through 90° to release a door bolt.
When the code sequence is incorrect the red LED will flash briefly.
The pressed key codes are also sent out to the serial moniter to make it easier for debugging purposes. This part of the sketch can be edited out of the final sketch otherwise it may compromise system security.

```
// Code_lock.ino

#include <Password.h>
#include <Keypad.h>
#include <Servo.h>

Servo myservo;
Password password = Password( "123456" ); // change password here!

const byte ROWS = 4; // Four rows
const byte COLS = 4; // columns
char keys[ROWS][COLS] =
{ {'1','2','3','A'},
  {'4','5','6','B'},
  {'7','8','9','C'},
  {'*','0','#','D'}
};
byte rowPins[ROWS] = { 4, 5, 6, 7 };
byte colPins[COLS] = { 8, 9, 10, 11};

Keypad keypad = Keypad( makeKeymap(keys), rowPins, colPins, ROWS, COLS );

const byte LEDred = 12, LEDgreen = 13, ServoPin = 2;

const int openTime = 1000;

void setup()
```

```
{ Serial.begin(9600);
  delay(200);
  pinMode(LEDgreen, OUTPUT);
  pinMode(LEDred, OUTPUT);
  myservo.attach(ServoPin);
  keypad.addEventListener(keypadEvent);
}

void loop()
{ keypad.getKey();
  myservo.write(0);
}


void keypadEvent(KeypadEvent eKey)
  { switch (keypad.getState())
    { case PRESSED:
      Serial.print("Enter: ");
      Serial.println(eKey);
      delay(10);
      if(eKey == char('A'))
      { checkPassword(); delay(1);
      }
      else password.append(eKey); delay(1);
    }
}

void checkPassword()
{ if (password.evaluate())
  { // password ok
    Serial.println("Accepted"); delay(10);
    myservo.write(90);
    digitalWrite(LEDgreen, HIGH); delay(openTime);
    digitalWrite(LEDgreen, LOW);
    password.reset(); delay(1);
  }
  else
  { // password NOT ok
    Serial.println("Denied"); delay(10);
    myservo.write(0);
    digitalWrite(LEDred, HIGH); delay(openTime);
    digitalWrite(LEDred, LOW);
    password.reset(); delay(1);
  }
}
```

Chapter 9 • Principles of Arduino Programming

One of the main reasons for the success of the Arduino platform is its super-simple programming environment. The Arduino IDE (**I**ntegrated **D**eveloping **E**nvironment) is very easy to use, even youngsters with no previous experience can have their own programs up and running in no time.
In addition the IDE supports libraries of routines for almost every application. This facility makes it much easier to get your own project working quickly. It's not necessary to start from scratch and reinvent the wheel every time, you can select from a wide range of tried and tested library routines written by other programmers.

For building your own projects it will undoubtedly be helpful to have some background understanding of the Arduino programming language. A brief introduction covering the most important commands is therefore included in the following chapters.

This introduction is not intended as a basic course but as a reference which should help to explain any parts of a sketch which are not immediately clear.

For a more comprehensive introduction check out the bibliography (chapter 14).

The basic program structure

Any Arduino program or 'sketch' consists of two sections:

1. void setup() {   instructions; }

2. void loop() {   instructions; }

The **setup** is executed first when a program starts running; this section is only executed once and serves to initialize things like the GPIO pin modes and to set up a serial communication channel for example.

After the setup() function comes the loop() function. This section contains the main part of the program code. This is executed repeatedly in an endless loop.

Functions

A function is a block of code which has its own name. When the function is called by its name the instructions contained within it will be executed. Also void setup() and void loop() are nothing more than special functions provided by Arduino's programming system.

Creating your own functions is useful to simplify repetitive tasks and to improve the readability of the program structure. First off you will need to define the type of function. This is determined by the data type of the value returned by the function. For example if the function returns a value which will be an integer, the function type is 'int'. When the function does not return any value the function type is 'void'. After the function type is defined the function name comes next then curly braces or brackets:

```
Typ FunctionName(parameter)  {    instructions;  }
```

Syntax elements

{} curly braces

Curly braces are used to denote the beginning and end of functions, loops and conditional statements.

; Semicolon

A semicolon marks the end of a statement.

/*... */ A comment block

Multi-line comments are text areas that contain no program code but only descriptions of a program section. They begin with /* and end with */. They can extend over as many lines as necessary.

// one-line comment

Comments that just take up just one line begin with a double forward slash //.

Variables and Variable declaration

Variables can be assigned different values during program execution, unlike constants which keep the same value during program execution.

A variable must be declared before it is used. A initial value can also be assigned to it.

```
int value1 = 0;
```

The Arduino system includes some reserved constant names:

HIGH/LOW	Defines pin output state
INPUT/OUTPUT	Defines pin as input or output function
true/false	false = 0, true = not false

Data types

The following data types are available in the Arduino-IDE:

boolean	*TRUE or FALSE*
char	-127 to 127
unsigned char	0 to 255
byte	*0 to 255*
int	-32,7678 to 32,767
unsigned int	0 to 65,555

word	0 to 65,555
long	-2,147,483,648 to 2,147,483,647
unsigned long	0 to 4,294,967,295
float	-3.4028235E+38 to 3.4028235E+38
double	-3.4028235E+38 to 3.4028235E+38

Arrays

An Array or field is a collection of variables that can be accessed using an index number which represents their position in the array. The first position in the array has the index number 0.

```
int myArray[] = {value0, value1, value2...}
```

To use a value stored in the array you can assign its value to a variable by using a statement which points to its position in the array. For example the value stored in the fourth position of an array called myArray is assigned to x:

```
x = myArray[3];
```

Arithmetic

The arithmetic operators are Addition, Subtraction, Multiplication and Division. example:

```
y = y + 3; x = x - 7; i = j * 6; r = r / 5;
```

With these operations the original data type will also apply to the result so that 9 / 2 will give the result 4 and not 4.5. The values 9 and 4 are integer variables and therefore whole numbers. When the result of the operation is greater than the maximum value allowed then an overflow occurs.

These logical operators are also available:

&	bitwise and
|	bitwise or
^	bitwise xor
~	bitwise not
<<	Shift Left
>>	Shift Right

Compound Operators

The compound operators are a sort of shorthand code to perform a mathematical or logical operation:

Function		example	meaning
--	decrement	*x--*	*x = x - 1*
+=	compound addition	*x += 2*	x = x + 2
-=	compound subtraction	*x -= 2*	x = x - 2
*=	compound multiplication	*x *= 2*	x = x * 2
/=	compound division	*x /= 2*	x = x / 2
%=	compound modulo	*x %= 2*	x = x % 2
&=	compound and	*x &= 2*	x = x & 2
|=	compound or	*x |= 2*	x = x | 2
^=	compound xor	*x ^= 2*	x = x ^ 2
<<=	compound shift left	*x <<= 2*	x = x << 2
>>=	compound shift right	*x >>= 2*	x = x >> 2

Program flow control

if...else:

This gives you control over the program flow. It allows multiple tests to be grouped together allowing several conditions to be tested:

```
if (SensorValue < 500)
  { // Executes when
  // SensorValue is less than 500
  }
else
  { // Is executed in all other cases,
  // can be omitted
  }
```

for:

This is the classic loop instruction:

```
for (initialization; condition; increment)
  { //instructions;
  }
```

Start condition: 'initialization'
Test condition: 'condition'
Count steps: 'increment' or 'decrement'

The loop

```
for (int i = 1; i<=10; i++)
```

will assign the values from 1 to 10 to the variable i.

switch case:
Switch/case is used to test the value of a variable in accordance to the case statements enclosed in curly braces. When the value of a case statement matches the variable, the code in that case statement is run.

The function is controlled by the following parameters:

var	Variable tested
default	This is optional, it is executed when nothing else matches
break	Without break the switch statement will go on to execute following expressions which may not be required.

Example:

```
switch (var)
  { case 1: // will be executed when var == 1
  break;
  case 2: // will be executed when var == 2
  break;
  default: // if nothing else matches the default is executed
    }
```

while()
While-loops will execute continuously until the expression in the parenthesis becomes false.

```
while(logic expression)
  { // instructions
  }
```

example:

```
var = 0;
  while(var < 99)
  { // This instruction will be executed 99 times
    var++;  // Compound instruction for var = var + 1
  }
```

do ... while()
The do...while loop works similarly to the while loop. The difference is that here the condition to loop is tested at the end of the loop.
The do...while loop will therefore always be executed at least once.

```
do
{ // Instructions
```

```
    }
    while (exit condition);
```

Example:

```
    var = 0;
    do
    { // Instructions
      var++;
    }
    while (var < 99);
```

break

Using break you can exit any do-, for-, or while loop.

Example:

```
    for (x = 0; x < 100; x ++)
     { // instructions;
     z = 2*y;
     if (z > 50)
      { // Exit the loop when z becomes bigger than 50
      break;
      }
    }
```

Timing control

unsigned long millis()

Returns the number of milliseconds that have elapsed since the current program started. Note that after 2^{32} ms = 4294967296 ms = 4294967.3 s = 1193.04 h = 49.71 days, i.e. almost 50 days, the value of this variable reaches maximum value, overflows and and starts from zero again.

delay(ms)

Introduces a delay in ms (Milliseconds).

delayMicroseconds(µs)

Introduces a delay in µs (Microseconds).

Mathematical Functions

The Function

```
min(x, y)
```

decides which of the two values is the smallest and returns that value.

Similarly

```
max(x, y)
```

decides which of the two values is the largest and returns that value. Overview:

```
abs(x)
```

computes the absolute value of a number or value. The functions

```
pow(x,y)

sqrt(x)
```

are used to raise a value to a power and find the square root of a value. Trig functions such as

```
sin(x)
cos(x)
tan(x)
```

are also implemented in Arduino

Serial Communication

Using Serial.begin(baudrate) opens the serial communication port. The data rate or baud rate is also defined by the command. The default baud rate for communicating with the Serial Monitor of the IDE on the computer is 9600 baud.

The following standard baud rates are also supported:

300
1200
2400
4800
9600
19200
38400
57600
115200

Example:

```
void setup()
  {    Serial.begin(9600);
  }
```

Opens the serial interface and sets the data rate to 9600 bps.

NB: Serial communication takes place using Arduino pins D00 und D01. When serial communications are used in an application the digital pins 0 (RX) and 1 (TX) have limited availability for other uses. It is adviseable to only use these two pins as general I/Os when there are no other pins available.

Using the instruction

```
Serial.println(data)
```

Sends data to the serial port. Print has the suffix 'ln' which adds a carriage return and line-feed control character to the end of the data. This makes sure the cursor jumps back to the start of the next line ready for the more data.

using

```
Serial.print()
```

Omits the control characters.

Chapter 10 • Use of Libraries

The availability of libraries or LIBs and their ease of use are an essential reason for the success of the Arduino system. LIBs are not a new idea; they have been around a long time in other programming environments also. The earlier versions usually incurred a license fee and were not generally known about, whereas the Arduino libraries are free.
It's fair to say that with the advent of the Arduino IDE, this situation changed fundamentally. A variety of standard libraries are already provided free of charge when you install the IDE. More importantly, however, a whole host of various LIBs have been developed by the world-wide community of Arduino users. These libraries are always available free of charge on the Internet.
Thus, a comprehensive set of applications is now available to the general public. In most cases there is a suitable LIB for every planned project or program application.

In most cases, the library can be loaded as a ZIP file from the Internet.
To do this, the ZIP file is first unzipped then the new file directories are copied into the directory using this path:

arduino-x.y.z\libraries

After a restart the library will be installed and ready to use.

Alternatively you can just go to the tab Sketch -> Include Library and Add .ZIP library... then find the file location and double click on the ZIP file to include it. The library manager is also available to check which libraries are installed and also to install additional libraries.
The following is a list of all the libraries used in this book. Sometimes it's possible that a link is no longer active. In this case it is usually easy to find an alternative by using a search engine.

Keypad library:

http://playground.arduino.cc/Code/Keypad#Download

LiquidCrystal-I2C-library:

https://github.com/fdebrabander/Arduino-LiquidCrystal-I2C-library

Seven-segment display:

http://sim.marebakken.com/SevenSeg.zip

Time library:

https://github.com/PaulStoffregen/Time

Temperature/humidity sensor DHT11:

http://arduino.cc/playground/Main/DHTLib

Infra-red remote control:

https://github.com/shirriff/Arduino-IRremote

RTC Module library for the DS130 timer chip

https://github.com/msparks/arduino-ds1302

RFID module:

https://github.com/miguelbalboa/rfid

Password:

http://playground.arduino.cc/Code/Password

IR remote control:

https://github.com/shirriff/Arduino-IRremote

Chapter 11 • Fault finding

I guess you're here because a project does not work as expected; this section may help. The following points summarize the most common causes of error. Take a methodical approach and go through, ticking them off one after the other. By the time you have finished there a good chance you will have tracked the problem down.

- Some components will only work properly if they are connected the right way round. Check all these 'polarized' components especially the electrolytic capacitors, IC's and LEDs.
- Ensure there are no accidental shorts between connection wires or component leads.
- Double check that all the resistors are the correct value. The color code bands are sometimes difficult to read under poor or artificial lighting. 1 Kohm and 10 Kohm resistors are often incorrectly identified. A digital voltmeter with a resistance range is useful here to check a resistor value.
- When power is supplied from batteries install a new set to make sure they are up to the job. As the supply voltage drops too low it can produce unusual and unreliable operation.

For building Arduino projects the simplified overview diagrams shows what plugs in where and how everthing connects together. This works well when you are just getting started but for larger layouts with several modules it can be a bit confusing. It sometimes helps if you revert to standard circuit diagram symbols and then draw in the connections. This is a kind of reverse-engineering approach which will give you a better understanding of the circuit and help spot a wrong connection.

Chapter 12 • Components and Modules

This book is principally designed to be used together with the RF-ID kit. All of the projects and experiments can be carried out using components supplied in the kit. There may be some people particularly interested in building just a few of the projects described here.

In this case it's possible to order the components needed for the projects of interest. In this next chapter we identify the components and suggest where they could be obtained.

The descriptions also help you track down suitable replacements if any item gets lost or becomes defective.

Breadboard

Standard prototyping breadboards are available in several different sizes. The one supplied with the kit is relatively large with lots of room to build circuits.
The smaller boards are also useful for less complicated projects. The boards are available from online stores and also high street component stockists.

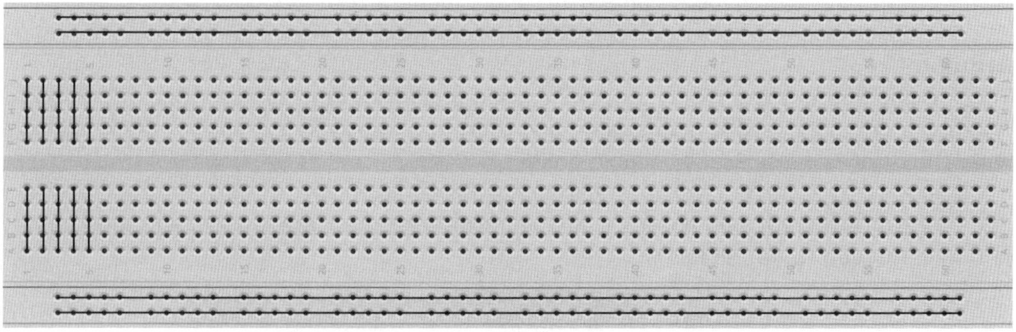

Illustration 98: A protyping breadboard

Resistors

Resistors are available form all stockists of electronics parts. The kit is supplied with:

- 10 x 220 Ohm resistors,
- 10 x 1 K-ohm resistors,
- 10 x 10 K-ohm resistors

It often works out cheaper to buy a bulk pack containing all the standard values rather than buying individual values.

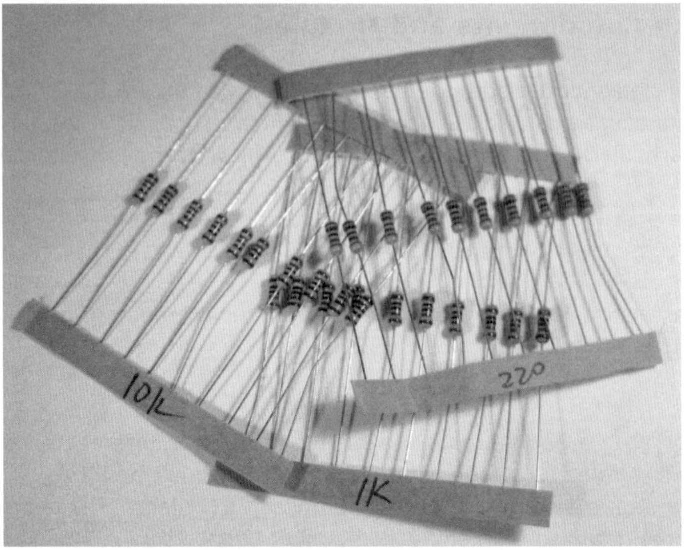

Illustration 99: An assortment of resistors

Arduino

The Arduino board is the main component used in all the projects described in this book. A genuine original board is high quality and therefore relatively expensive, there is also a wide choice of clone-boards available online.

The range of Arduino-clone boards available form SainSmart are low-priced, good quality and have proved to be reliable.

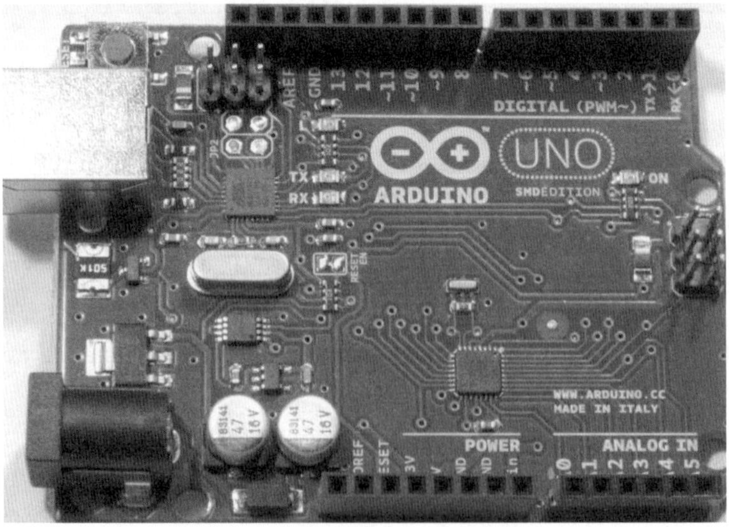

Illustration 100: The Arduino Uno

USB cable

USB cables are common enough; you probably already have a few spare cables kicking around, if not check your local supermarket. For the Arduino you need a simple cable with a type A connector at one end and a type B connector at the other. They are also available from online stores.

Illustration 101: USB cable

Light Emitting Diodes

Light emitting diodes or LEDs are amongst the most easily recognizable components in electronics. They are widely available from online sellers and high street component stockists and come in every imaginable shape and size.

- 5 red
- 5 yellow
- 5 geen

LEDS should be enough to get you started. They are very cheap and available in all imaginable shapes and sizes; it's always worth having a few spares of different sizes. They are also available in mixed bag assortments which work out very economical.

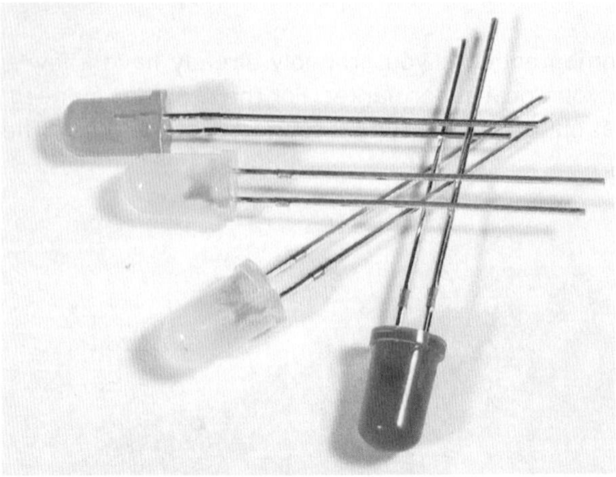

Illustration 102: LEDs

Jumper cable

Jumper cables are used to make reliable connections between header socket strips and prototyping breadboards without the need for soldering. The most common type has a short length of exposed stiff wire at each end with a flexible insulated wire in between. You can also use lengths of appropriate-diameter single-strand cable with the ends stripped. This works out cheaper but is not quite so convenient.

The kit also includes a short length of ribbon cable with 10 male, pin terminations at one end and 10 female sockets at the other end. These are useful to make connections to header pins on modules and the prototyping board. They can also be used to make connections between the leads of individual components and the Arduino.

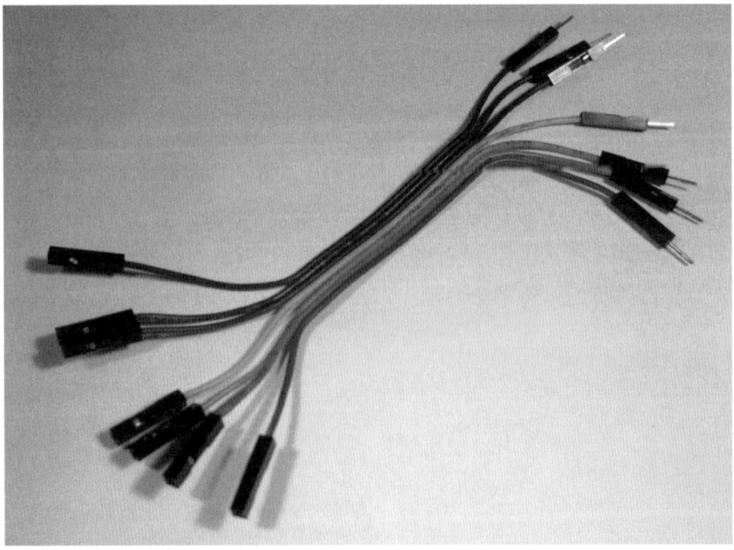

Illustration 104: Male-Female cable

Both types of cable are widely available in various colors from online stores and high street component stockists.

LC Display

Liquid Crystal Displays (LCD) are available in lots of different forms. The majority of displays for Arduino applications use the HD 44780 controller chip and can be written to using parallel data transfers. The display used throughout this book however has an additional module incorporated which requires only two control lines. This additional I2C module connects directly to the pins of the display unit. This type of unit is not quite so common but is available as a complete unit from some online stores. They tend to be more expensive than the standard displays using parallel data loading.

It is also possible to wire up HD44780 compatible display to the Arduino.
Another alternative is to purchase the I2C module separately and solder it to the row of connections on the LCD but you first need to be sure that they will work together successfully.
This option would probably be recommended for the more experienced user.

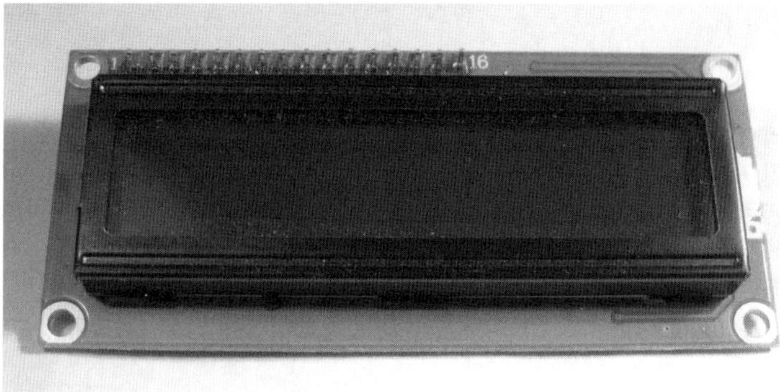

Illustration 105: LC Display

RFID module

The module used here is known as the

- RFID-RC522

and is available from many online stores at low cost. Any customization of the the module is difficult because it uses SMD components that have been soldered professionally into place.

Illustration 106: The RFID module

White card and Key fob tags

Examples of RFID cards and key fobs tags are usually supplied along with the reader module. Additional tags can also be ordered online. Another format for the tag is a sticky label with integrated RFID electronics. You can also use the reader module to scan any other tags you may have lying around.

Illustration 107: White card and key fob tags

Joystick module

Joystick units are available from many electronic suppliers as single units or as a complete module. Very high quality units are also available as spares for model radio control transmitters but these are quite expensive. The simpler, low-cost version is more than sufficient for the majority of applications.

Illustration 108: The Joystick module

Keypad module

The Keyboard module consists of 16 pushbuttons wired together as a 4 x 4 matrix. It can be made up using 16 individual pushbuttons wired together in the same way as the matrix. Complete keypad modules are also available; some have numbers printed on the key caps.

Illustration 109: The Keypad module

RTC module

The RTC module is available from a number of online shops also. The module is based on the

- DS1302

real time clock chip. This can also be purchased on its own. In addition to the IC you only need a backup battery and a clock crystal to build your own RTC module on a breadboard.

Illustration 110: The RTC module

Water level sensor

Water level sensors are produced by a number of different manufacturers.
When an identical sensor cannot be found, a compatible replacement should be available.
It may be necessary to make changes to the corresponding sketch.

As mentioned earlier in the sketch, this type of sensor tends to become unreliable after prolonged use. It's worth seeking out a more robust design for long term reliability.

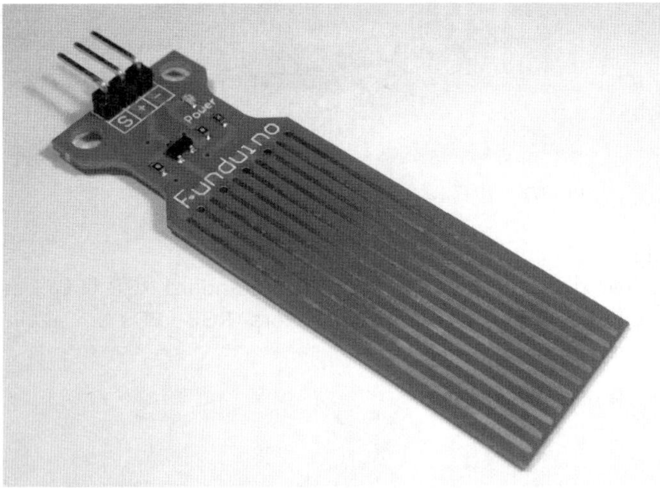

Illustration 111: The water level sensor

Humidity/temperature sensor

This module is relatively difficult to obtain but essentially just consists of the double-sensor type

- DHT11

This sensor on its own is available from many online stores. You just need an additional resistor to use it on a breadboard.

Illustration 112: Humidity/temperature sensor

RGB LED module

The RGB LED module can simply be replaced by a standard RGB LED. The only additional components you need are the three series resistors. RGB LEDs are available widely from most component suppliers.

Illustration 113: The RGB LED module

Stepper motor and motor drive module

Both the stepper motor and the matching driver module are available from several online retailers. Other motors can also be used. The driver IC used in this module is the

- ULN2003

This chip can is available from many suppliers and can be fitted directly onto a breadboard by the more experienced user.

Illustration 114: The stepper-motor driver module

Illustration 115: The stepper-motor

Relay module

Relay modules are available from many online stores. Alternatively there are also versions of the relay driver which plug directly into a mains outlet. These have the advantage that they can be safely used by amateur builders to switch mains voltage loads and feature fully isolated 5 V input switch control signals.

Illustration 116: Relay module

Microphone module

The microphone module like this or similar can be ordered online from a number of suppliers. Alternatively builders with some knowledge of analog electronics can build a simple microphone preamp.

Illustration 117: The microphone module

Potentiometer 10k

Potentiometers come in all shapes and sizes. A pot with a resistance value of 10 K Ohm is suitable for the applications here. These are also widely available from component distributors.

Illustration 118: The 10k Potentiometer

Seven-segment display
The single seven-segment display included in the kit has the part number

- 5161AS

This is a very common component, available from many electronic suppliers.
Other types of display can also be used but it may be necessary to make changes to the sketch to drive other types of displays successfully.

Illustration 119: A seven segment display

4x7-segment display
The 4 x 7-segment display has the part number

- SH5461AS

The same comments apply to this display as for the single 7-segment display. These displays are also available using other color LEDs, these can also be used here instead of the display with red segments.

Illustration 120: 4x7segment LED displays

LED matrix
LED matrices are relatively specialized components. There are many different variants available, the matrix we use in this book has the part number

- SH1388ASR

These are available from online stores and any other compatible matrix can also be used but it may be necessary to change the associated sketch.

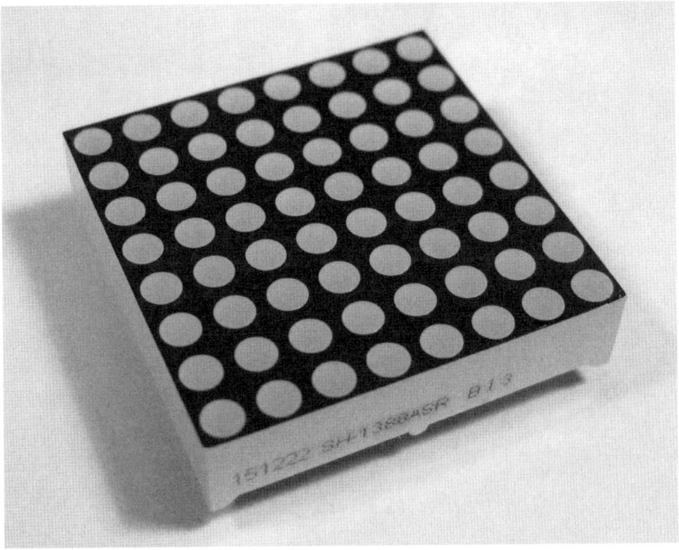

Illustration 121: 8x8 LED matrix

Servos

The type of servos we use here are available from hobby model shops and online. They are classed as micro servos and are quite cheap.

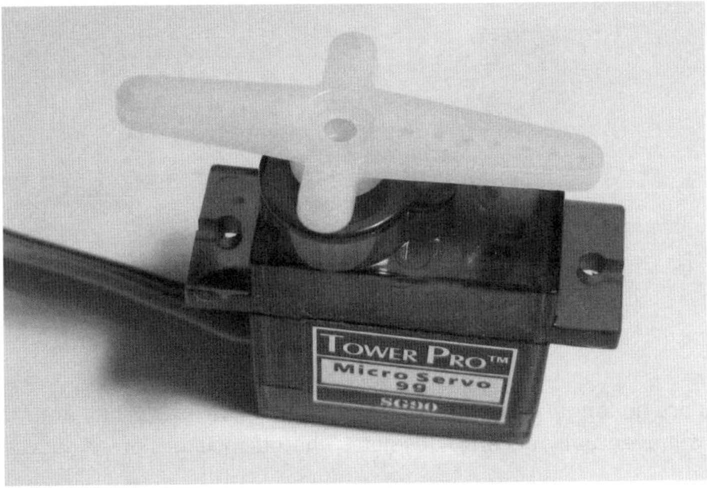

Illustration 122: A micro servo

Piezo speaker

Piezo speakers are common components that you can order from many online component suppliers. Make sure that the component you order is the speaker alone without any extra circuitry. Speakers with additional integrated electronics are not suitable for use with experiments described in this book.

Illustration 123: The piezo speaker

Tilt switch

Tilt switches are available from many online suppliers. Even though they come in different shapes and sizes they all perform similarly and can be used with the kit.

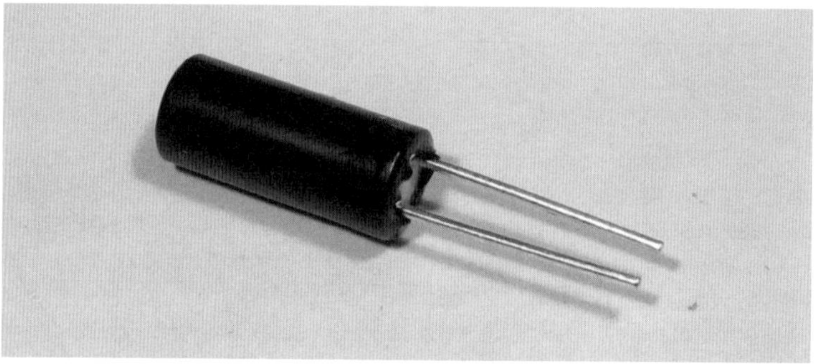

Illustration 124: The tilt switch

Photo resistor

Photo resistors are no longer completely state of the art devices. They are made from toxic materials and will eventually become obsolete. Phototransistors are a good substitute, use a

- BPW40

or equivalent component.

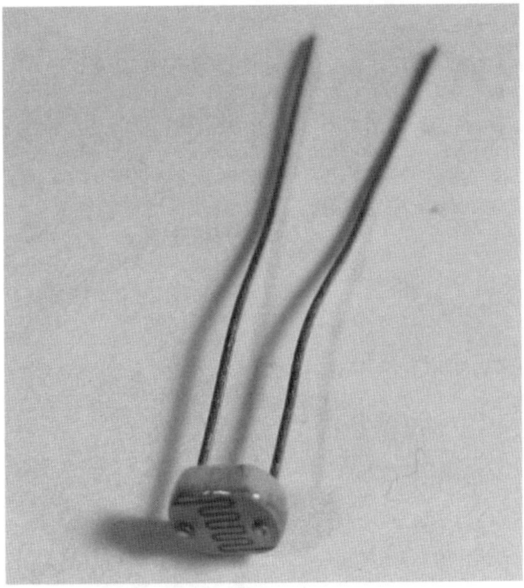

Illustration 125: A photo resistor

Pushbutton

There are many different types of pushbuttons. It always useful to have a few spares, they can be used for all sorts of applications. The usual online suppliers have a wide range to choose from.

Illustration 126: Pushbutton

9V Battery clip

Battery clips are widely available. It's more difficult to find one with the correct barrel plug to fit the Arduino socket.

It may be necessary to buy the clip and correct-sized plug separately and then solder the cable yourself.

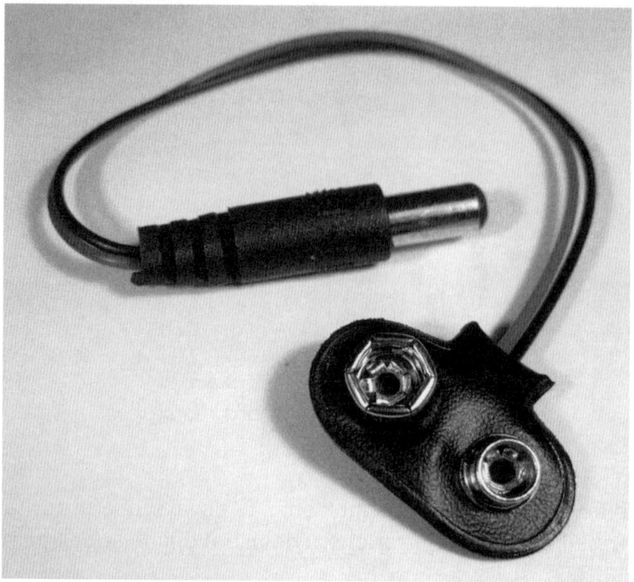

Illustration 127: 9 V battery clip

IR-Flame sensor

The flame sensor is also a discrete component which is relatively easy to source. An infra-red diode can also be used here. A possible substitute type is the

- SFH 203 FA

Which is widely available online.

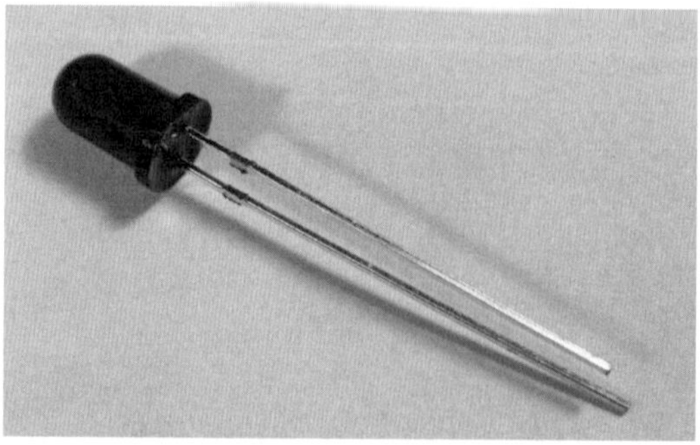

Illustration 128: The flame sensor

IR receiver and IR remote controller

Remote control receiver chips are stocked by the usual component stockists. There are many different types available. The IR receiver chip supplied with the kit has the part number

- VS1838B

This particular part is relatively difficult to find, the TSOP31238 from Vishay is an alternative part but it has a different housing and the pinouts are differently arranged so it would be necessary to study the data sheets for these two components.

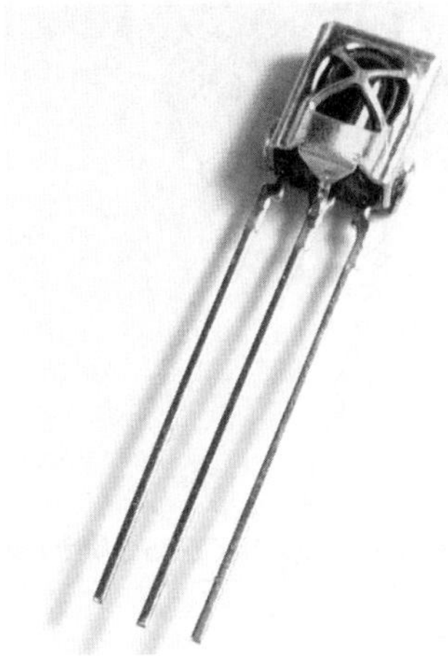

Illustration 129: The IR receiver

As well as using the hand held remote controller supplied with the kit, many other remote controllers can also be used to send signals to the IR receiver.   You just need to check if the controller and receiver are compatible.

Illustration 130: The IR remote controller

IC 74HC595

The 74HC595 is a standard shift register type IC. It can be sourced from online shops for a few pennies, make sure you order the standard DIL leaded package that plugs into an IC socket and not one of the SMD types.

Illustration 131: IC 74HC595 shift register

The LM35DZ temperature sensor

The LM35DZ is also a standard component stocked by the majority of component suppliers.

Illustration 132: The LM35DZ temperature sensor

Component suppliers

As you become more proficient you will want to add to the modules and components supplied with the kit. You may also need to replace an item that has gone missing or been damaged. These components are available from a large number of electronic suppliers, many of which use online auction sites. Recommended suppliers include:

1) Mouser Electronics: www.mouser.com
2) Conrad Electronics: www.conrad-electronic.co.uk

Some of the online stores such as Amazon and Ebay have suppliers who often supply bundles of components and various different modules and expansion boards which represent good value.

Chapter 14 • Literature

This book is aimed directly at users of the RFID starter kit for Arduino and inlcludes projects which use the components supplied in the hardware kit. Working through the chapters will give you a good grounding in the basics of electronics and guide you through the construction of some useful and practical projects. For further study to reinforce your knowledge we suggest the following publications:

[1] P. Horowitz, W. Hill; The Art of Electronics, 3rd Edition (2015)
[2] G. Spanner; Arduino - Circuits & Projects Guide (2012)

Chapter 15 • Illustration Listing

Index